MATHEMATICAL STUDIES

A Series for Teachers and Students

EDITED BY

DAVID WHEELER

University of Leicester

No. 1

TRANSFORMATION GEOMETRY

In the same series

No. 2

ALGEBRAIC STRUCTURES

by A. W. Bell

No. 3

VECTORS

by E. H. Leaton

No. 4

SETS AND BOOLEAN ALGEBRA

by M. Rueff and M. Jeger

In preparation

INTRODUCTORY TOPOLOGY by J. E. Reeve

LOGIC by W. O. Storer

Transformation Geometry

By

MAX JEGER

Oberrealschule, Lucerne

ENGLISH VERSION BY

A. W. DEICKE AND A. G. HOWSON

University of Southampton

London

GEORGE ALLEN AND UNWIN LTD

RUSKIN HOUSE MUSEUM STREET

FIRST PUBLISHED IN ENGLISH IN 1966
SECOND IMPRESSION 1969
THIRD IMPRESSION 1970

Translated from the German
KONSTRUKTIVE ABBILDUNGSGEOMETRIE

Cloth edition I SBN 0 04 513002 7
Paper edition I SBN 0 04 513003 5

REPRODUCED AND PRINTED IN GREAT BRITAIN
BY REDWOOD PRESS LIMITED
TROWBRIDGE & LONDON

FOREWORD

It is generally agreed that school mathematics syllabuses are in need of reform. The traditional syllabus is no longer an adequate preparation for mathematics as it is taught at a higher level; it indicates very little of the range of contemporary uses of mathematics; and it contains a high proportion of routine computation and manipulation at the expense of mathematical ideas which yield immediate enjoyment and satisfaction. A number of schools are now experimenting with new syllabuses which attempt to cure these faults.

Whether the experiments prove to be wholly successful or not, they are bringing a new element into the situation: an awareness that it is part of the job of the teacher of mathematics to inform himself about the relatively recent developments and changes in his subject. It is no longer possible to believe that developments in mathematics concern only the research mathematician and do not have any bearing on the mathematics taught in schools. This series of books is intended as a contribution to the reform of school mathematics by introducing to the reader some areas of mathematics which, broadly speaking, can be called modern, and which are beginning to have an influence on the content of school syllabuses.

The series does not put forward explicit advice about what mathematics to teach and how it should be taught. It is meant to be useful to those teachers and students in training who want to know more mathematics so that they can begin to take part in the existing experimental schemes, or modify them, or devise their own syllabus revisions, however modest. The books are elementary without being trivial: the mathematical knowledge they assume is roughly that of a traditional grammar school course, although substantial sections of all the books can be understood with less.

Now that the stability over a long period of school mathematics syllabuses seems to be coming to an end, it is to be hoped that a new orthodoxy does not succeed the old. The reform of mathematics teaching should be a continuing process, associated with a deepening study of the subject throughout every teacher's professional life. These books may help to start some teachers on that course of study.

D.W.

PREFACE TO THE THIRD GERMAN EDITION

The teaching of mathematics in grammar schools today is in an unsettled state. Transformation geometry, which has recently been introduced into school syllabuses, is the outcome of a series of reforms which have aimed at liberating the teaching of geometry from domination by Euclid.

The traditional teaching of geometry is based on Euclid in two ways. First, logic always takes precedence with Euclid; the arrangement of the material is essentially determined only by logic. Theorems are put next to each other if an abstract logical proof is possible, without regard to whether they belong together, or whether they are essential or unimportant. Secondly, the Euclidean style in teaching is distinguished by its emphasis on rigid figures; rigid congruence of triangles is considered to be the main method of proof in elementary geometry.

The notion of transformation gives to modern teaching of geometry a central concept comparable to the idea of function in analysis. The hierarchy of groups of transformations leads to a natural order for the material, and instead of the static treatment of Euclid we have a dynamic geometry.

Although transformation geometry dates back to Felix Klein (1849-1925), this reform is still fully in keeping with modern tendencies which demand that, in our teaching, more emphasis be placed on mathematical structures and isomorphisms. Only in one respect can it be called old-fashioned—it seeks to preserve geometry as an essential part of mathematical teaching.

The first two editions of this book produced a series of hints and proposals for furthering the use of transformation geometry in the classroom. Their aim was to make a larger circle of teachers familiar with these new ideas. The third edition has been completely revised. It has been extended into a course on transformation geometry which has been tried out several times during the last few years by the author in his own teaching. The general arrangement of the former editions, which built up theory and applications from concrete examples, has been preserved. The range of problems has been considerably extended.

PREFACE TO THE THIRD GERMAN EDITION

Reforms will only prove acceptable if they leave open various ways of access from previous teaching. For this reason a too rigidly systematic representation has been avoided. This course presupposes some previous knowledge of geometry; it is assumed that the pupil knows the elementary parts of congruence and similarity geometry.

Our book differs to some degree from previous school books on transformation geometry since it makes much more use of the group-theoretic structure of elementary geometry. Algebraic operations for transformations are introduced at an early stage and are afterwards used extensively as a method of proof. We should like to throw open to discussion the question 'to what extent is this algebraic approach to school geometry likely to give the pupil more insight into the subject?' In the final sections an attempt has been made to build a bridge from constructive geometry to analytic geometry.

The axiomatic system behind this course has, intentionally, not been discussed consistently. The author is convinced that in school teaching axiomatic discussions can at most have a local or retrospective character. But in the latter respect they belong to the advanced sixth form stage.

The diagrams have been drawn by two pupils, A. Schenk and R. Ronchetti, from Lucerne. Dr. H. Loeffel has helped by reading the proofs. The author is most grateful to all these helpers.

Lucerne, September 1963.

CONTENTS

TRANSLATORS' NOTE

A bibliography of texts written in English on transformation geometry would hardly impress the casual reader by its length. Yet, although books on the subject are not numerous, there is already a wealth of notation and nomenclature available to budding authors. While preparing this version we have constantly been faced with the need to choose between alternative names for a particular transformation and the choice has not always been easy. For example, 'half-turn' is an admirable description of a rotation through 180°, but by adopting this name one loses the line-point analogy and, what is perhaps more important, a means of considering the transformation in a way that can be easily generalized to three dimensions. In this instance, as elsewhere, we have used the term which is most likely to have been encountered by schoolteachers. The general similarities are not so well known as the isometries and here we have followed Coxeter in the use of 'spiral similarity'. Since we have preferred 'enlargement' to 'dilatation' (or 'dilation', for spelling provides an additional degree of freedom), we have not used 'dilative reflection' but have added 'stretch-reflection' to the geometer's vocabulary. We would plead in defence that the name is self-explanatory and can be usefully compared with 'glide-reflection'.

One major change in notational practice has been made for this version. Textbooks recently published in England have tended to prefer the 'functional order' for the product of transformations, that is, TR is to be interpreted as *first* the rotation R and *then* the translation T. We have followed this convention which seems to have much to commend it.

A.D., A.G.H.

LIST OF SYMBOLS

$E(S,\mu)$	an enlargement with centre S and scale factor μ
H_O	a half-turn about the point O
M_s	a reflection in the line s
$R(O,\theta)$	a rotation about the point O through the directed angle θ
T	a translation
$W(S,\theta,\mu)$	a spiral similarity with centre S, angle of rotation θ and scale factor μ
Z	a stretch-reflection
$\Phi(s,\alpha,\mu)$	a perspective affinity with axis of affinity s, direction α and scale factor μ
$\mathfrak{A}$ (A)	the group of enlargements
$\mathfrak{B}$ (B)	the group of translations and rotations
$\mathfrak{B}'$	the group of translations and half-turns
$\mathfrak{K}$ (K)	the group of plane isometries
$\mathfrak{Q}$ (Q)	the group of affine transformations
$\mathfrak{Q}_s$	the group of perspective affinities with the given axis s
$\mathfrak{S}$ (S)	the group of spiral similarities
$\mathfrak{S}^*$	the group of similarities
$\mathfrak{T}$ (T)	the group of translations

1

MAPPINGS

We introduce the idea of a mapping by means of a simple example. Select one point S in the plane. For every point A we can find a point A' such that the line segment AA' has its mid-point at S. This condition ensures that a unique point A' is associated with A. Moreover, if A runs through all the points of the plane, then so does A'. Here we have a *mapping of the plane onto itself.* If we wish to give this relation a definite direction, then we call A the *original*, or *object*, point and A' the *image* point.

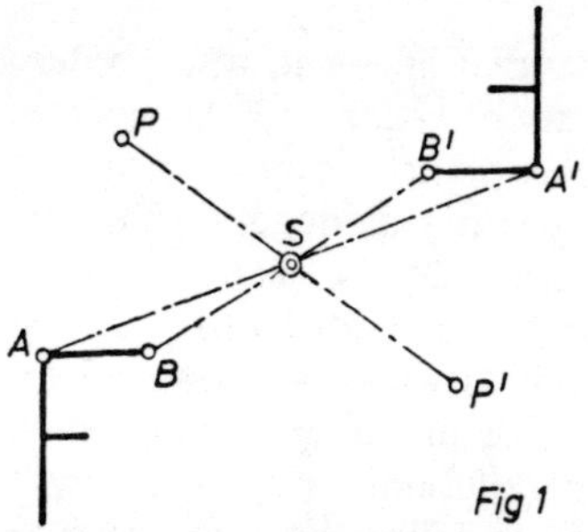

Fig 1

If for every given object point A there is exactly one image point A', and if for every given point B' there is exactly one original B—that is, if the mapping is unique in both directions—then the mapping is called *one-one*. Our example has this property; here the *inverse mapping*, that is, the mapping which maps the image back onto the original point, is given by the same rule of construction.

This example illustrates a very special type of mapping. The notion of mapping, however, includes every correspondence

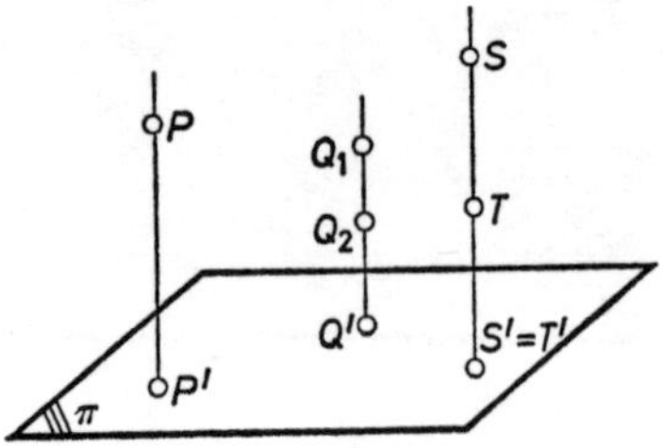

Fig 2

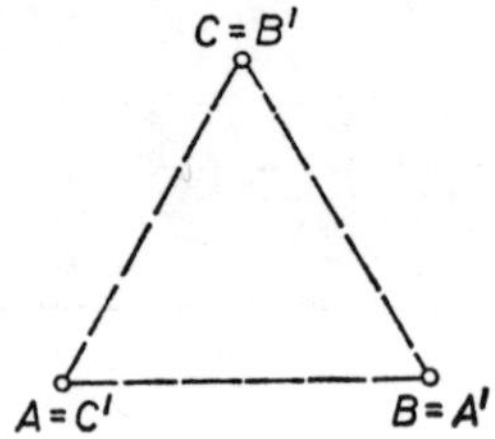

Fig 3

between sets of geometric objects. We shall give a rough outline of the range of possible mappings by means of a few further examples.

Let α and α' be two planes in space. A pencil of parallel lines (the lines being parallel neither to α nor to α') produces a correspondence between the points of intersection with α and α'. This unique mapping is called a *parallel projection* from α onto α'.

A pencil of parallel lines can also define a correspondence between the points of space and the points in a plane π. We associate with every point P in space the point of intersection of π with the line passing through P. This is called a parallel projection of space onto the plane π. In this mapping every point P in space has a unique image P'; however, there are infinitely many points which are mapped onto any particular image point Q'. The mapping is uniquely defined but is not one-one. If the parallel lines are perpendicular to the plane π, then the mapping is called the *orthogonal projection* of space onto the plane π (see Figure 2).

The sets related by a mapping may contain different types of objects. For example, mappings between a set of points and a set of lines, or a set of points and a set of circles are considered in higher geometry.* When we draw plans and elevations of an object then we are mapping points in space onto a suitable set of triples of points in the plane.

Similar correspondences between sets are also of great importance in other fields of mathematics. For example, the

* Examples are poles and polars and cyclographic mappings.

function $f: x \rightarrow y$ defines a correspondence between the variables x and y. Let us consider $y = x^2$. This defines a correspondence between the real numbers in the two intervals $-5 < x < 5$ and $0 \leqslant y < 25$. It is easily verified that this correspondence is not one-one. However, the same function defines a one-one correspondence between the sets $\{x:1 < x < 5\}$ and $\{y:1 < y < 25\}$. If these sets of numbers are illustrated geometrically by point sets on two lines, we can consider the function to be a mapping. So we see that functions and mappings are related ideas.

When 24 pupils sit in a classroom with 24 chairs, then we have a one-one correspondence between the set of pupils and the set of chairs. Here the correspondence is between finite sets. Mappings between finite sets also occur in geometry. For example, a rotation through 120° about the centre of an equilateral triangle ABC maps the vertices onto each other in the following way: $A' = B$, $B' = C$, $C' = A$ (see Figure 3). Here we have a mapping of the finite set $\{A,B,C\}$ onto itself. One-one mappings of a finite set onto itself are called *permutations*.

In this monograph we shall consider almost exclusively one-one mappings of the set of all points in the plane onto itself. We shall use the word *transformation* to describe this type of mapping.

The transformations of the plane onto itself which are considered in elementary geometry can all be based on constructions with compass and ruler. This course develops some topics of plane geometry using these transformations as a basis.

2

REFLECTION IN A LINE

Let s be some selected line in the plane. Let us now imagine that all the points of the plane are traced onto a sheet of transparent paper. If we turn this sheet over in such a way that every point originally on s coincides with its original position, then we obtain a correspondence between points of the plane by transferring the points from the tracing paper back onto the plane. We call this mapping of the plane onto itself a *reflection in the line s* and we denote it by the symbol M_s.* We shall call s the *axis* of reflection.

Reflection in a line is a transformation having the following obvious properties on which we shall base our further investigations.

1. To every line s there corresponds a reflection M_s. If A' is the image of A under M_s, then A is the image of A' (see Figure 4(a)). We write

$$M_s(A) = A', M_s(A') = A.$$

2. The points of s remain in the same position; they are the *fixed points* of the mapping M_s. We say that s itself is a fixed line of the mapping. If A is not on s, then A' lies on the opposite side of s. The line AA' is also a fixed line; it is, however, not pointwise fixed like s (see Figure 4(a)).

3. The reflection M_s preserves straight lines, that is, a straight line, g, has as its image another straight line, g' (see Figure 4(a)).

* We here follow the current British notation; that is, we shall denote rotations by R and reflections by M (for mirror).

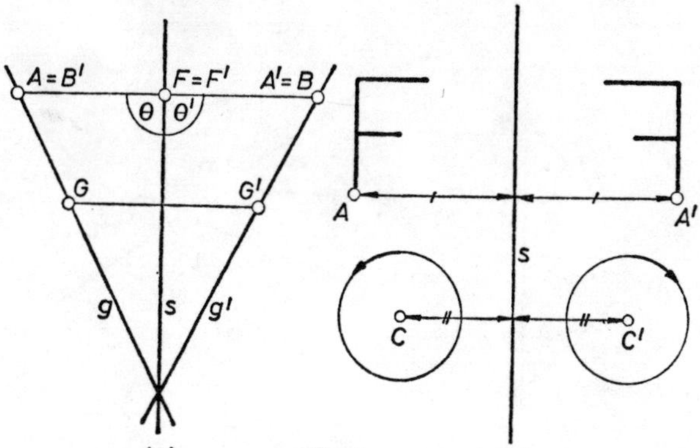

(a) Fig 4 (b)

4. The reflection M_s leaves distances and angles invariant. A closed polygon and its image, however, have opposite orientation (see Figure 4(b)).

A particular consequence of 4 is that the angles θ and θ' shown in Figure 4(a) are equal. This implies that AA' and s are perpendicular lines.

Together with the relation $AF = A'F$ this gives a simple construction for obtaining images under the reflection M_s: the line segment joining corresponding points A and A' is perpendicular to s and is bisected by it.

5. If two different points A and A' are given arbitrarily, then there exists exactly one reflection M_s such that $M_s(A) = A'$ and $M_s(A') = A$. The axis s is the mediator of the segment AA'.

6. Given two rays FA and FB issuing from a point F, then there exists exactly one reflection M_s interchanging the two rays. The axis s is the bisector of the angle AFB.

Problem 1. Given s, a point A, $A' = M_s(A)$, and a point X, construct the image point X' using only a ruler (that is, only straight lines may be drawn).

Hint: remember that if $B = A'$, then $B' = A$. Every pair of corresponding points, therefore, defines a second pair.

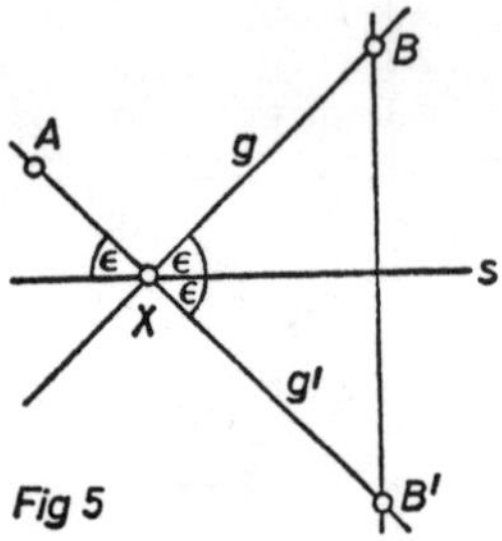

Fig 5

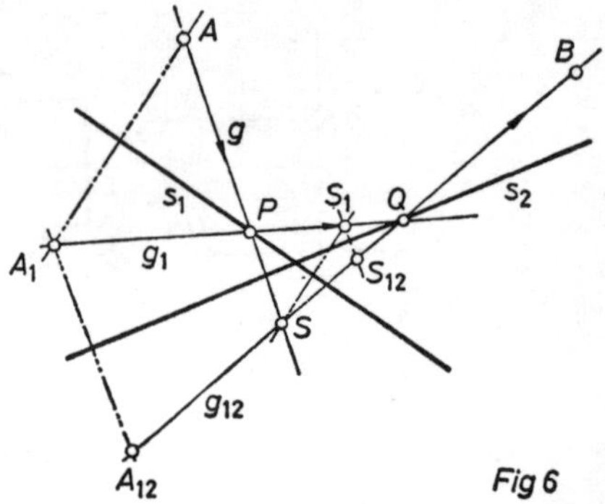

Fig 6

Problem 2. Given are a line s and two points A and B on the same side of s. Find the point X on s for which the length of the path composed of the two line segments AX and XB is a minimum.

Imagine the segment XB reflected in s. Its length is not changed, that is, we have

$$AX+XB = AX+XB'.$$

We can immediately find the minimum of $AX+XB'$; it is given by the segment AB'. The two parts AX and XB of the minimal path lie on symmetric lines g and g' (see Figure 5). The point X is characterized by the fact that the two lines intersect s in three equal angles.

According to *Fermat's principle*, light follows the path for which the time of travel is a minimum. In a homogeneous medium minimum time of travel is equivalent to minimum distance travelled. Reflection of light in a plane mirror, therefore, leads to Problem 2. Figure 5 provides a basis for the solution by construction of many problems on reflection.

Problem 3. A ray of light issuing from a point A is to be reflected in two lines s_1 and s_2 in such a way that it finally passes through a given point B (see Figure 6).

The solution can be developed from that given for Problem 2. Now, however, we must make two reflections.

In the solution shown in Figure 6, A has first been reflected in

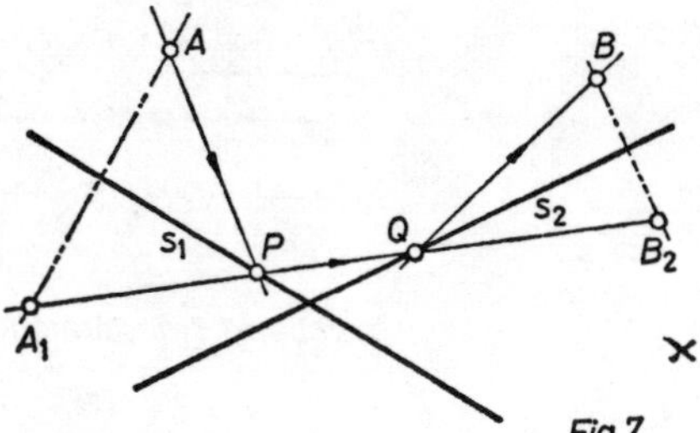

Fig 7

s_1 and its image A_1 mapped onto A_{12} by reflection in the line s_2. Another possible method of solution is shown in Figure 7. Here B has been mapped onto B_2 by reflection in the line s_2. In both constructions the line segments drawn (namely, $A_{12}B$ and A_1B_2) have the same length as the path of light from A to B. It should be mentioned that while the problem always has a geometrical solution this does not mean that there is always a sensible physical solution. For example, for a solution to have any physical meaning the two points of reflection P and Q must lie above the intersection of the lines s_1 and s_2.

We now return to Figure 6. Reflection in s_1 maps g onto g_1 which is mapped onto g_{12} by reflection in s_2. We may take g_{12} as being obtained directly from g if we interpret the result of performing the two reflections, one after the other, as a new transformation. This expresses an essential idea of transformation geometry: *transformations can be combined.* The result of this composition is a new transformation.

In order to clarify this idea we now consider the combination of two reflections away from our particular construction problem. We map the points of the plane first by the reflection M_a in a line a, and then map the images obtained by a reflection M_b. The correspondence between a point A and its final image $A_{12} = M_b(M_a(A))$ defines a new transformation which we shall denote by M_bM_a. Note that this notation indicates the order of composition as '*first* M_a, *then* M_b'—as is usual with functional notation we read from right to left. Figure 8 illustrates the construction of this new mapping.

The process of combining transformations just described is

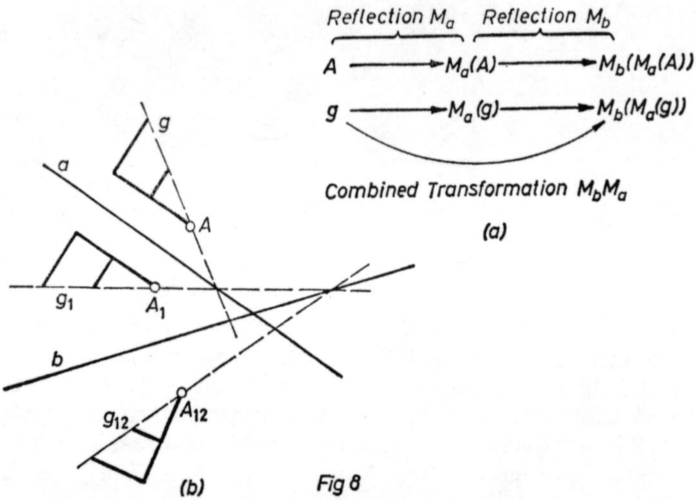

Fig 8

not restricted to reflections in lines; it produces from two arbitrary transformations Φ and Ψ a new transformation $\Psi\Phi$. This symbol means that each point is first mapped by Φ, then its image is mapped by Ψ.

Now we can see that the set of all mappings of the plane onto itself has a property we have already met in algebra. Combination of transformations is an operation associating with any two transformations a new transformation, that is, an object of the same kind. We find a similar situation, for example, with the set of all positive numbers if we consider multiplication as the operation of composition. By stressing these analogies our geometric considerations will assume an algebraic aspect.

If a reflection M_s is performed twice, we obtain the mapping

$$M_sM_s = M_s^2,$$

which leaves all points of the plane in the same position, that is, every point of the plane is a fixed point. This trivial mapping is called the *identity transformation* and it is denoted by the symbol I. In the set of all transformations, I plays a similar part to that of the number 1 in the set of numbers mentioned above; for every transformation Φ we have

$$\Phi I = I\Phi = \Phi.$$

Definition. If we reverse the correspondence between points given by a transformation Φ, we obtain the *inverse transformation* to Φ. This is denoted by Φ^{-1}.

It follows from this definition that, for every transformation Φ,

$$\Phi\Phi^{-1} = \Phi^{-1}\Phi = I.$$

Definition. Any transformation (other than the identity) which is the same as its inverse is called an *involutory mapping* or *involution.*

From $\Phi^{-1} = \Phi$ we deduce that an involution satisfies the equivalent relation

$$\Phi\Phi = \Phi^2 = I.$$

Reflections in lines, therefore, are examples of involutions.

Problem 4. Show by means of suitable drawings:

(a) M_pM_q is not, in general, the same transformation as M_qM_p, that is, the combination of reflections is *non-commutative*;

(b) $M_pM_q = M_qM_p$ if p and q are orthogonal lines.

Figure 9(a) illustrates the first assertion.

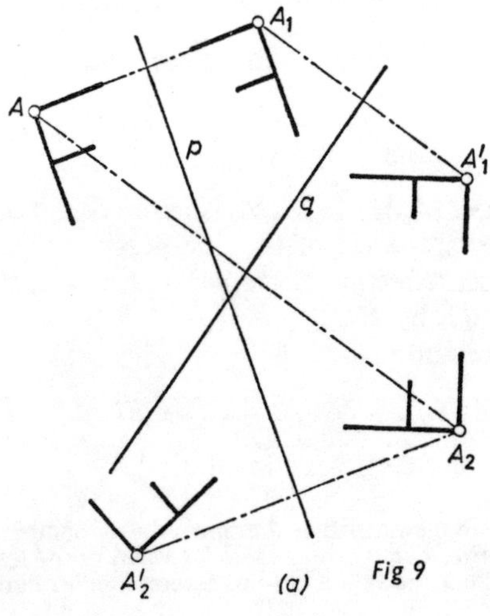

(a) Fig 9

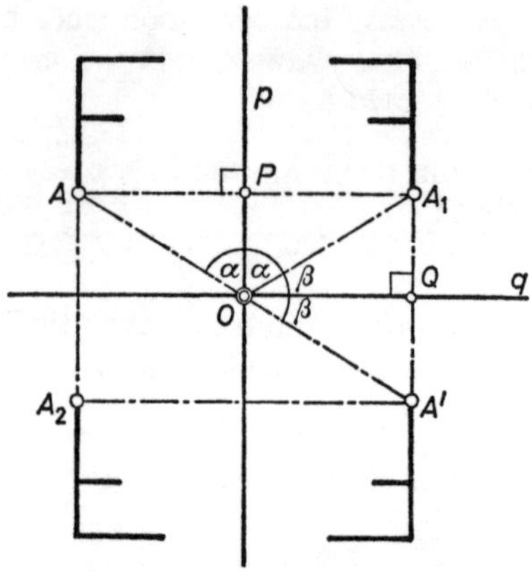

Fig 9 (b)

So as to prove the second assertion, we show that every point A is mapped by the combined transformation onto the same image irrespective of the order in which the reflections are carried out (see Figure 9(b)).

$$\underset{M_qM_p}{A \underset{M_p}{\longrightarrow} A_1 \underset{M_q}{\longrightarrow} A_1'} \qquad \underset{M_pM_q}{A \underset{M_q}{\longrightarrow} A_2 \underset{M_p}{\longrightarrow} A_2'}$$

From the invariance of distances and angles we deduce

$$\left.\begin{array}{l} A, O, A_1' \text{ are collinear and } OA_1' = OA \\ A, O, A_2' \text{ are collinear and } OA_2' = OA \end{array}\right\} \Rightarrow A_1' = A_2' = A'.$$

The mapping $M_pM_q = M_qM_p$ is easily constructed if we note that O is the mid-point of the line segment AA'. We call this transformation *reflection in the point O* or a *half-turn about O* and we denote it by H_O.

From the relation

$$H_O^2 = H_OH_O = M_pM_qM_qM_p = I$$

we see that a half-turn is an involution.*

* We have here assumed that the operation of combining transformations is *associative*, that is, that $(M_pM_q)(M_qM_p) = M_p((M_qM_q)M_p)$. The reader should check the validity of this assumption for himself.

In connection with this problem we want to mention briefly the question of parallels. The quadrangle $AA_1A'A_2$ is obviously a rectangle. However, we can only prove this if we use some axiom which expresses, in some form or other, Euclid's postulate on parallels. If we want to base plane geometry on the study of transformations, the following postulate appears to be especially suitable.

If three angles in a quadrangle are right-angles, then so is the fourth angle. (Axiom of the existence of the rectangle.)

From this we deduce that the quadrangle OPA_1Q is a rectangle. The same is true for the three other quadrangles in corresponding positions. But then we have proved that all the angles in the quadrangle $AA_1A'A_2$ are right-angles.

Problem 5. Show that for every rectangle there exist two reflections M_p and M_q which map the rectangle onto itself. The axes p and q are orthogonal.

Definition. If a reflection M_p maps a figure onto itself, then we say that p is an *axis of symmetry* of the figure. If the figure is mapped onto itself by a half-turn H_O, then we say that O is a *centre of symmetry* of the figure.

Figure 10 shows two reflections which map the square $ABCD$ onto itself, the axes of symmetry being s_1 and s_2. The square has four axes of symmetry; a regular n-sided polygon is easily shown to have n axes of symmetry. For a circle every diameter is an axis of symmetry.

Wallpaper patterns, especially friezes, supply us with many simple examples of figures with infinitely many axes or centres

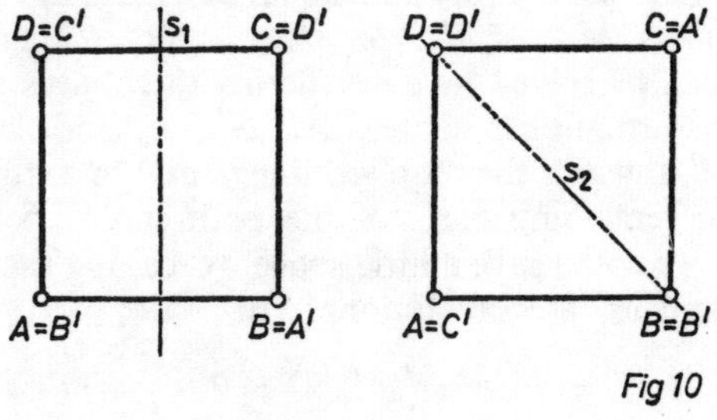

Fig 10

of symmetry. (We must here assume that the pattern is extended indefinitely.)

Definition. Two lines g and h are called *parallel* if both are orthogonal to a line a.

It is easy to deduce from this that parallel lines are also characterized by the equality of a pair of alternating angles with a line a.

Problem 6. Deduce from the definition that:

$$f \| g \text{ and } g \| h \Rightarrow f \| h.$$

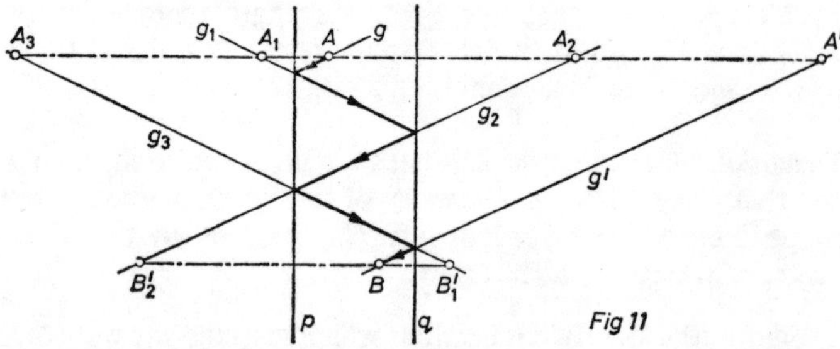

Fig 11

Problem 7. We are given two parallel lines p and q and two points A and B between them. We wish to construct the path of a ray of light issuing from A which passes through B after being reflected twice in both p and q, the first reflection being in p.

Let g be the line along which the light begins to travel. Then the subsequent parts of the path lie on the image lines of g under the mappings M_p, M_qM_p, $M_pM_qM_p$ and $M_qM_pM_qM_p$. The problem can be solved by constructing the images of A under these transformations, namely A_1, A_2, A_3 and A'. The line through A' and B is the required line g' and once this has been drawn the remaining parts of the path can be found easily. Note that we could save a little space by making use of the fact that M_p and M_q are involutions. For

$$M_qM_pM_qM_p(g) = g'$$

and, therefore,

$$M_pM_q(M_qM_pM_qM_p(g)) = M_pM_q(g').$$

But, using the involution property,

$$M_pM_qM_qM_pM_qM_p(g) = M_qM_p(g).$$

That is, we can obtain g_2 by considering the line joining $A_2 = M_qM_p(A)$ to $B_2' = M_pM_q(B)$. This obviates the need to construct A'.

Problem 8. Solve Problem 7 if only three reflections are demanded (for example, one in p and two in q).

Problem 9. A rectangle has width p and length $2p$. The sides of the rectangle lie on the lines a, b, c and d, and its centre is M. Construct the hexagon MA_1BCDA_2 with A_1 and A_2 on a, B on b, C on c and D on d, which has the smallest perimeter subject to these conditions. Express this minimal perimeter in terms of p.

We can solve the problem by considering the image of M under the transformation $M_aM_dM_cM_bM_a$.

However, we prefer to split this chain into the products $M_cM_bM_a$ and M_aM_d: this leads us to the two points $M_3 = M_cM_bM_a(M)$ and $M_2' = M_dM_a(M)$ (cf. Problem 7). The

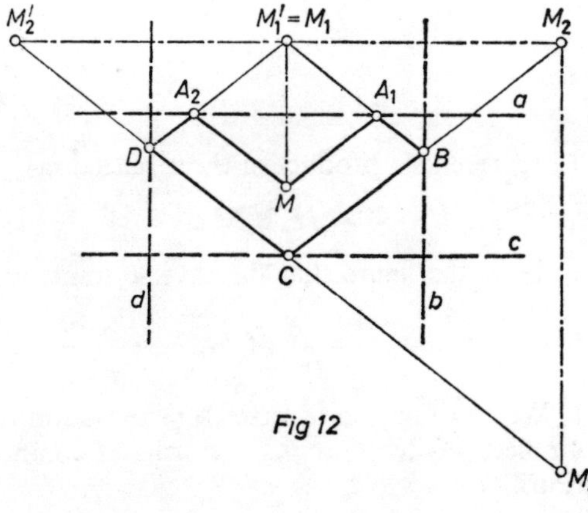

Fig 12

minimal perimeter is equal to the length of M_3M_2'. We find that it is $5p$.

If we consider the symmetry of this problem, we can see immediately that C is the centre of a side of the rectangle. If C is known the construction can be considerably simplified.

In the solutions of Problems 3, 7, 8 and 9 we have met products of a finite number of reflections. These are transformations leaving distances and angles unchanged. Hence, if a figure is mapped by a product of a finite number of reflections, then its image is congruent to the original.

Definition. Finite products of reflections are called *congruences* or *isometries*.

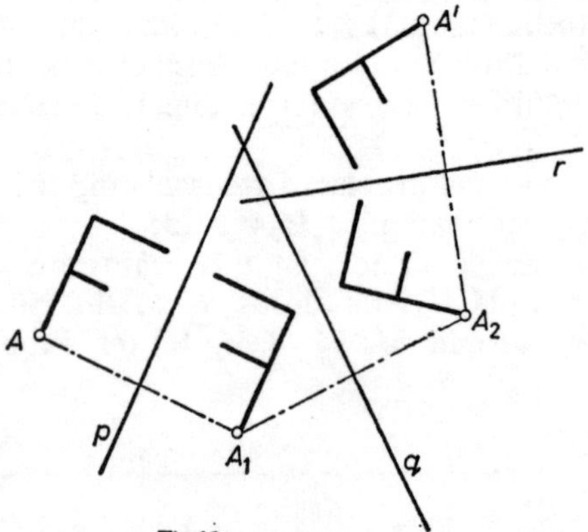

Fig 13

Figure 13 represents a product of three reflections

$$\Phi = M_r M_q M_p.$$

We can see from the figure that the inverse transformation is given by

$$\Phi^{-1} = M_p M_q M_r.$$

Theorem 1. We can find the inverse transformation to a finite product of reflections by reversing the order of composition of the reflections.

After these remarks we turn to some further types of problems whose solutions can be found by means of reflections.

Problem 10. A line s and two circles Γ_1, Γ_2 are given. Construct squares with two opposite vertices on s and with one of the remaining vertices on each of the circles Γ_1 and Γ_2.

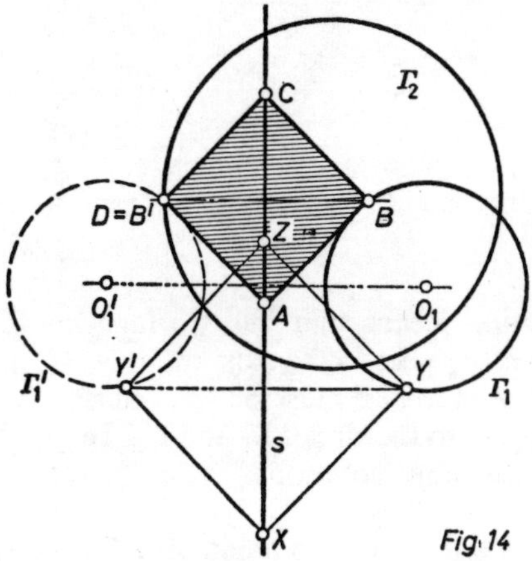

Fig. 14

Assume that A and C lie on s. The vertices B and D are then symmetrically placed with respect to s, that is, $M_s(B) = D$. Imagine all the squares that could be drawn with X and Z on s and Y on Γ_1. The locus of the vertices Y' would then be the image circle Γ_1' $(= M_s(\Gamma_1))$. The vertex of the square to be constructed must, therefore, be a point of intersection of Γ_1' and Γ_2.

This solution is based on the reflection of a locus of points. This is a new way of using mappings to help us to solve construction problems.

Problem 11. A line s and two circles Γ_1, Γ_2 on the same side of s are given. Construct a point X on s with the property that tangents from X to the two circles make equal angles with s.

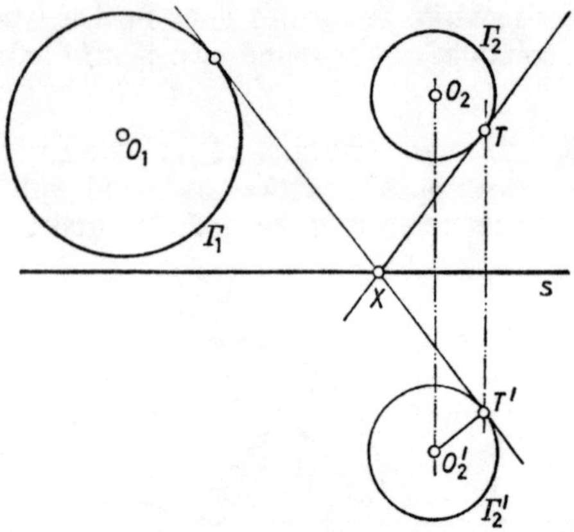

Fig 15

The condition means that the two tangents through X are symmetric with respect to the axis s, that is, M_s maps one onto the other. Therefore, X must be the intersection of s with a common tangent to the circles Γ_1 and Γ_2'. In general, therefore, the problem has four solutions.

Problem 12. A line g and two points A, B on the same side of g are given. Find a point X on g such that the angle between XB and g is twice as large as that between XA and g.

3

TRANSLATIONS

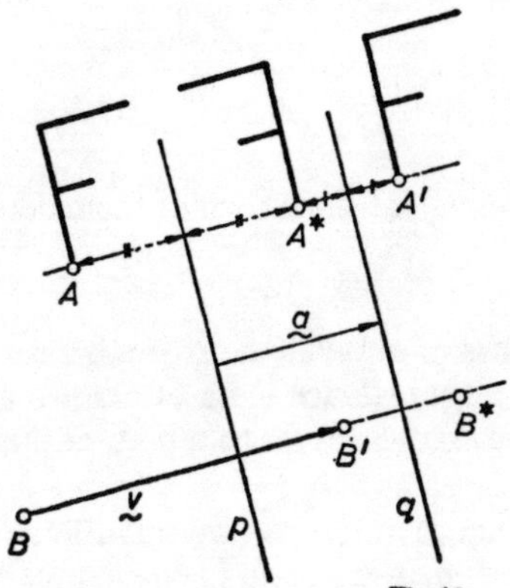

Fig 16

We now consider the product of two reflections in parallel axes p and q (see Figure 16).

$M_q M_p$ maps A onto the point A' on the perpendicular to p and q through A; the distance AA' being twice the distance between p and q. If we consider this new transformation without reference to M_p and M_q, we can characterize it as follows:

The lines joining corresponding points P and P' are parallel.

All points are moved the same distance in the same direction.

Definition. A mapping satisfying the above conditions is called a *translation.*

A translation is obviously determined if one arbitrary pair P, P'—consisting of a point and its image—are given. This pair determines a direction and a distance—two quantities which can be represented geometrically by an arrow leading from P to P'. The arrows associated with different pairs of corresponding

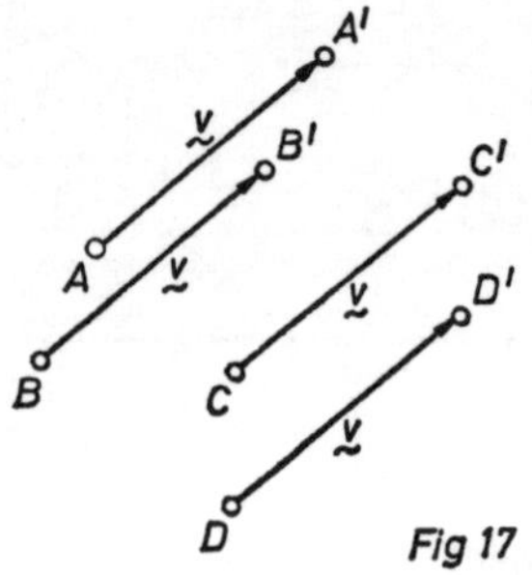

Fig 17

points are all equivalent since each of them determines the same translation.

Definition. A class of equivalent arrows is associated with every translation. The equivalence class of arrows is called a *vector*. Every one of the arrows serves to represent the vector.

We denote vectors in the text by small letters printed in bold type, for example, ***a***, ***b***, ***u***, ***v***, and in the figures by the symbol ~ placed below the letters.

If a translation is determined by a vector ***v***, we find the images of the points *A*, *B*, *C*, . . . by attaching the vector ***v*** to each of the points in turn (see Figure 17).

We now return to the generation of translations by composition of reflections (Figure 16). The translation resulting from the combination of M_p and M_q has a very simple relation to the lines *p* and *q*: the translation vector, ***v***, is twice as long as, and in the same direction as, ***a***, the vector perpendicular to *p* which runs from a point on *p* to a point on *q*. Here we have to note the order of composition; for the mapping M_qM_p the vector ***a*** points *from p to q*. We express the relation between ***v*** and ***a*** by the equation $\mathbf{v} = 2\mathbf{a}$.

We now consider a translation *T* with vector ***v***. If *p* and *q* are two parallel lines such that the vector ***a***, which is perpendicular to *p* and runs from *p* to *q*, satisfies the equation $\mathbf{a} = \frac{1}{2}\mathbf{v}$, then $T = M_qM_p$. Since there are infinitely many pairs of parallel lines which satisfy these conditions we have the following theorem.

Theorem 2. A translation T with vector $\boldsymbol{v}$ can be represented in infinitely many ways as a product of two reflections. The axes of the two reflections are parallel, are orthogonal to $\boldsymbol{v}$, and are a distance apart equal to half the length of $\boldsymbol{v}$.

We shall use this theorem to help us to analyse isometries.

It is obvious that translations, being products of reflections, are isometries. We deduce the following properties.

1. Translations are one-one mappings.

2. Translations are line-preserving transformations; moreover, the image g' of a line g is always parallel to g. (See Figure 18.)

3. Translations are *direct isometries*, that is, congruences which preserve orientation.

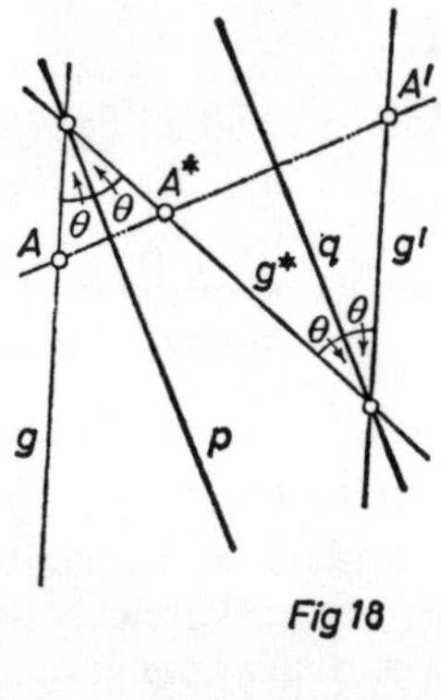

Fig 18

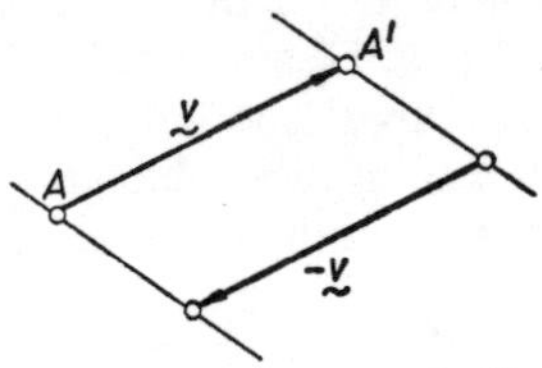

Fig 19

The inverse transformation to a translation T with vector $\boldsymbol{v}$ is again a translation. Its vector has the same length as $\boldsymbol{v}$, but opposite direction; it is denoted by $-\boldsymbol{v}$ (see Figure 19).

Before investigating translations further we shall consider two elementary constructions based on translation.

Problem 13. Two lines g and h are given. Construct a line x making an angle of 60° with g and such that its points of intersection with g and h are a distance d apart.

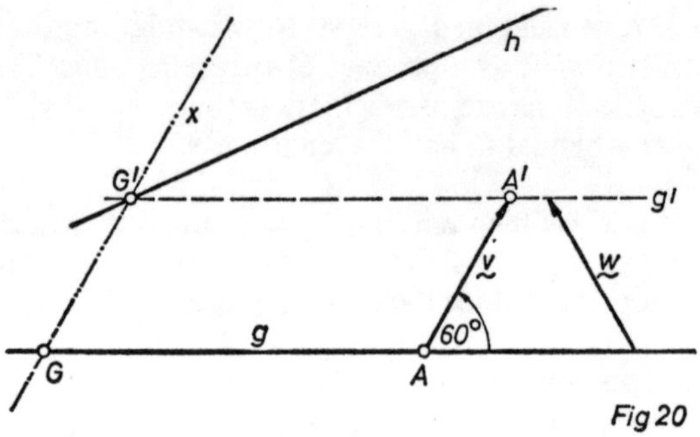

Fig 20

The angle of 60° with g and the length d determine a vector $\boldsymbol{v}$ (see Figure 20). A translation with vector $\boldsymbol{v}$ maps g onto g'. The required line x passes through the intersection of g' and h and is parallel to $\boldsymbol{v}$.

The problem has four solutions; it is easy to see that, apart from $\boldsymbol{v}$, the vectors $\boldsymbol{w}$, $-\boldsymbol{v}$ and $-\boldsymbol{w}$ will all lead to lines with the necessary properties.

Problem 14. Given are two circles Γ_1 and Γ_2 and a line g. Find a point A on Γ_1 and a point B on Γ_2 such that A and B are a distance d apart and AB is parallel to g.

Here a solution is obtained by mapping one of the circles by means of a translation with a vector $\boldsymbol{a}$ which is parallel to g and has length d.

COMBINATION OF TRANSLATIONS

When we consider the product of translations the half-turn, which was defined on p. 26, will prove to be an extremely useful aid and so we shall now consider this particular congruence in more detail.

First we show that a translation can be represented as the product of two half-turns. For this purpose we split the translation T into two reflections M_p and M_q (see Figure 21). If s is perpendicular to p and q, then

$$T = M_q M_p = M_q M_s M_s M_p = (M_q M_s)(M_s M_p)$$
$$= H_G H_F,$$

using the fact that the product of reflections in orthogonal lines

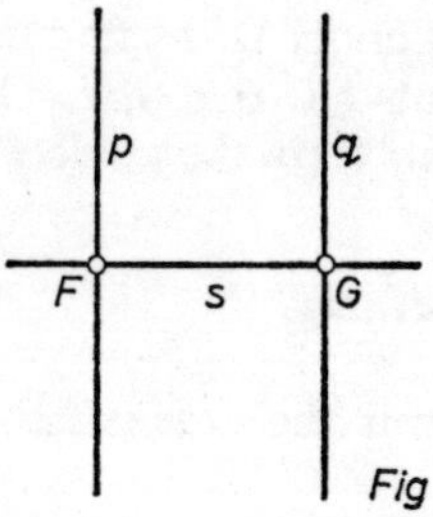

Fig 21

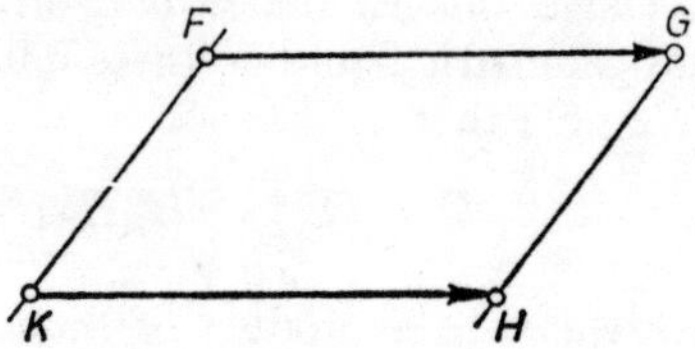

Fig 22

is a half-turn about their point of intersection.

We immediately deduce:

Theorem 3. A translation T with vector $\boldsymbol{v}$ can be represented in infinitely many ways as a product of two half-turns. The centres of the half-turns F and G have to be chosen in such a way that $\mathbf{FG} = \frac{1}{2}\boldsymbol{v}$.

Problem 15. Show that the product of three half-turns is again a half-turn.

Let the product be $\Omega = H_H H_G H_F$.

We solve the problem by considering the translation $H_G H_F = T$, which has the vector $\boldsymbol{v} = 2\mathbf{FG}$. Choose the point K such that $\mathbf{KH} = \mathbf{FG}$ (see Figure 22). Then we have

$$\Omega = H_H(H_G H_F) = H_H(H_H H_K) = H_K,$$

which proves our assertion.

Opposite sides of the quadrilateral $FGHK$ are parallel and of equal length. This can be shown by multiplying

$$H_G H_F = H_H H_K$$

by H_F on the right and by H_H on the left. We then obtain

$$H_H H_G H_F H_F = H_H H_H H_K H_F \Leftrightarrow H_H H_G = H_K H_F.$$

But this implies $\mathbf{GH} = \mathbf{FK}$. Hence the points F,G,H,K are the vertices of a parallelogram.

Remembering that a half-turn is an involution, we deduce the relation

$$\Omega^2 = H_H H_G H_F H_H H_G H_F = I.$$

Problem 16. Find the image of the point A under Ω^2 by finding successive images under half-turns about F,G,H,F,G,H. Of what geometric figure do these image points form the vertices?

We note that

$$\Omega = \Omega^{-1} \Leftrightarrow H_H H_G H_F = H_F H_G H_H.$$

Theorem 4. In a product of three half-turns the order of the factors may be reversed.

Problem 17. Let T be a translation with vector $\boldsymbol{v}$ and let H_F be a half-turn about F. Show that TH_F and $H_F T$ are also half-turns and construct their centres from $\boldsymbol{v}$ and F.

We now consider two translations T_1 and T_2 with vectors $\boldsymbol{a}$ and $\boldsymbol{b}$ respectively. We split each translation into two half-turns:

$$T_1 = H_G H_F, \; T_2 = H_H H_G.$$

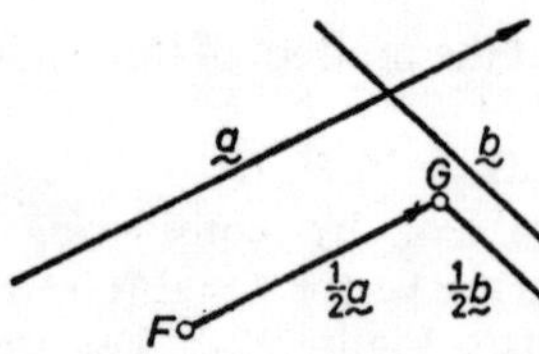

Fig 23

Combining T_1 and T_2 we obtain the mapping

$$T_2 T_1 = H_H H_G H_G H_F = H_H H_F,$$

which is clearly again a translation, being the product of two half-turns. On the other hand

$$\begin{aligned} T_1 T_2 &= H_G H_F H_H H_G = (H_G H_F H_H) H_G \\ &= (H_H H_F H_G) H_G = H_H H_F. \end{aligned}$$

Here we have used Theorem 4 which said that the order of factors in a product of three half-turns could be reversed.

Comparing the two representations for $T_2 T_1$ and $T_1 T_2$ we find

$$T_1 T_2 = T_2 T_1 = T.$$

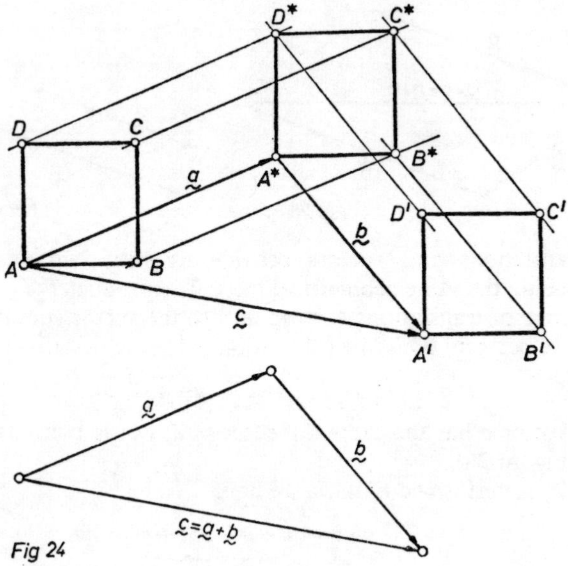

Fig 24

Theorem 5. The product of two translations is a translation. Moreover, the order of composition does not matter, that is, combination of translations is commutative.

We associate with the new translation T the vector $\boldsymbol{c}$. It can be obtained by considering the map of a single point A. The image of A under T_1 is A^* and T_2 maps A^* onto A'. The vector $\boldsymbol{c}$ is, therefore, represented by an arrow from A to A'. We call $\boldsymbol{c}$ the sum of the two vectors $\boldsymbol{a}$ and $\boldsymbol{b}$, and write

$$\boldsymbol{c} = \boldsymbol{a}+\boldsymbol{b}.$$

This associates with the operation of combining translations an operation defined for vectors which is called *vector addition*.

We obtain the vector sum of $\boldsymbol{a}$ and $\boldsymbol{b}$ by attaching the vector $\boldsymbol{b}$ to the 'point' of the vector $\boldsymbol{a}$. The vector sum is then the vector which starts at the starting point of $\boldsymbol{a}$ and ends at the end-point of $\boldsymbol{b}$ (see Figure 24). This construction appears to depend upon the order in which the addition takes place, but this does not influence the result since

$$T_2T_1 = T_1T_2 \Leftrightarrow \boldsymbol{a}+\boldsymbol{b} = \boldsymbol{b}+\boldsymbol{a} \qquad \text{(see Figure 25).}$$

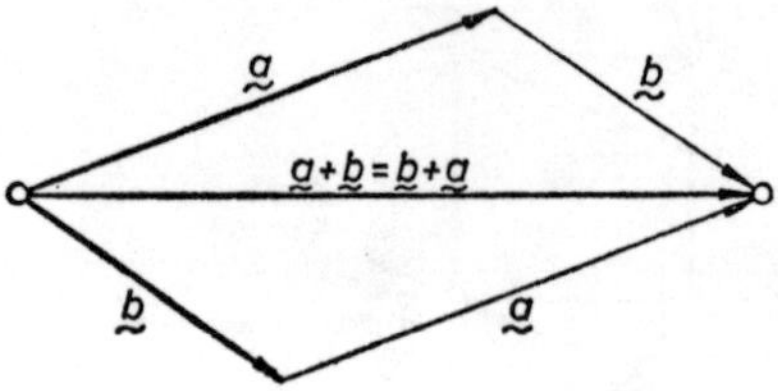

Fig 25

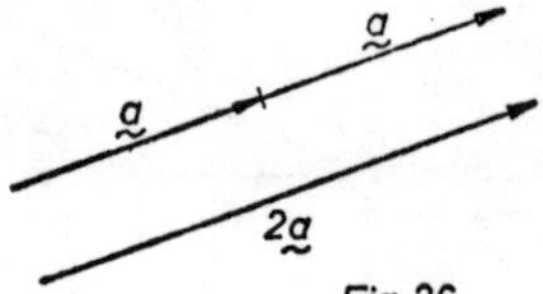

Fig 26

Translations and vectors provide us with two ways of expressing the same geometrical facts. The product T_2T_1 in the language of translations corresponds to the vector sum $\boldsymbol{a}+\boldsymbol{b}$.

If we perform the same translation twice, we describe this by

$$T = T_1T_1 = T_1^{\,2} \Leftrightarrow \boldsymbol{c} = \boldsymbol{a}+\boldsymbol{a} = 2\boldsymbol{a}.$$

The vector $\boldsymbol{c}$ has the same direction as $\boldsymbol{a}$, but is twice as long (see Figure 26).

If T_1 is performed n times, we have

$$T = T_1^{\,n} \Leftrightarrow \boldsymbol{c} = \underbrace{\boldsymbol{a}+\boldsymbol{a}+\ldots+\boldsymbol{a}}_{n \text{ times}} = n\boldsymbol{a}.$$

Here we have introduced the symbol $n\boldsymbol{a}$ for the vector which has the same direction as $\boldsymbol{a}$, but is n times as long.

For later applications we shall need the following generalization.

Definition. Let λ be a real number. We denote by $\lambda\boldsymbol{a}$ the vector with a length equal to the length of $\boldsymbol{a}$ multiplied by $|\lambda|$, and which has the same or the opposite direction as $\boldsymbol{a}$ according to whether λ is positive or negative.*

This definition includes the previously defined vector $-\boldsymbol{a}$; this is the vector $\lambda\boldsymbol{a}$ for $\lambda = -1$.

Certain geometric properties lead to further algebraic operations for vectors. The theory of these operations is called vector algebra. We are here only interested in vector addition

* The definition uses implicitly the following principle of continuity: if a line segment is given on a line, then every other segment on the line can be characterized by a real number: its measure in relation to the given line segment.

and in multiplication of vectors by a number. A further study of vector algebra is not, therefore, necessary for our purposes.

Vectors are of great importance in physics. Most physical quantities are vectors or similar to vectors. We mention as examples forces, velocities, accelerations, electric and magnetic fields.

GROUPS

We now consider the set $\mathfrak{T}$ of all translations. Included in this set is the *identity translation* which is interpreted as the translation with a vector of length zero.* We found that when two translations were combined the resulting transformation was again a translation (Theorem 5). Hence, when two elements of $\mathfrak{T}$ are combined they always yield another element of $\mathfrak{T}$. *The operation of composition does not take us outside the set* $\mathfrak{T}$. It has further been shown that associated with every translation there is an inverse transformation which is also a translation. *Every element of* $\mathfrak{T}$ *has an inverse which belongs to* $\mathfrak{T}$. Such sets with an operation defined upon them having the above properties are extremely important in modern mathematics. They are known as *groups*. So as to enable us to develop this idea we now give a precise definition of a group.

Definition. A set $\mathfrak{G}$ of objects (elements) $A, B, C, \ldots$ is called a group if the following postulates are satisfied.

I. An operation is defined on $\mathfrak{G}$ which associates with every ordered pair A, B of elements of $\mathfrak{G}$ a new element C which also belongs to $\mathfrak{G}$. C is called the product of A and B and we write

$$C = A\text{o}B.$$

II. There exists an element E of $\mathfrak{G}$ satisfying the relation

$$A\text{o}E = E\text{o}A = A$$

for all elements A of $\mathfrak{G}$.
E is called the *unit*, or *neutral*, element of the group.

* The direction of this vector is irrelevant. In vector algebra it is known as the zero vector.

III. For every element A of $\mathfrak{G}$ there exists an *inverse* element, denoted by A^{-1}, which satisfies

$$A \circ A^{-1} = A^{-1} \circ A = E.$$

IV. The operation is *associative*, that is,

$$(A \circ B) \circ C = A \circ (B \circ C).$$

Thus translations form a group when we take the operation of composition to be the result of performing the two mappings one after the other. The unit element is the identity translation. The inverse element corresponding to a translation with vector $\boldsymbol{v}$ is the translation with vector $-\boldsymbol{v}$. Postulate IV is automatically satisfied by the operation of combining transformations.

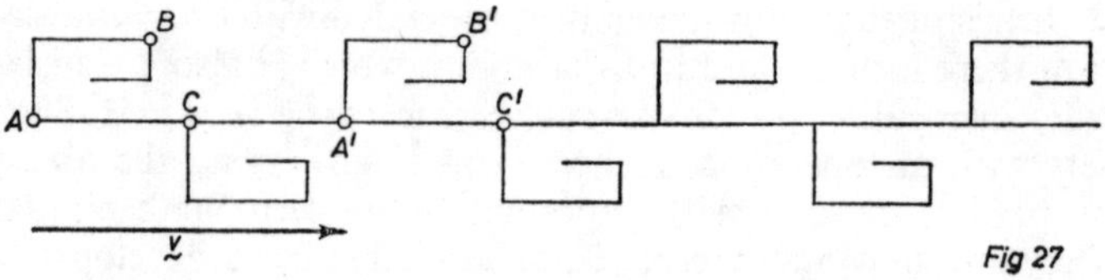

Fig 27

Further examples of groups of transformations may be obtained, for example, by considering only those translations which map a certain figure onto itself. Let us ask, for instance, which translations map the frieze pattern shown in Figure 27 onto itself. (We imagine that the pattern has been extended indefinitely in both directions.) One of them is certainly the translation with the vector $\boldsymbol{v}$. But the translations with the vectors $2\boldsymbol{v}$, $3\boldsymbol{v}$, $-\boldsymbol{v}$, $-2\boldsymbol{v}$, . . . also leave the figure unchanged. The figure, in fact, is left unchanged by any translation with a vector of the form $\lambda\boldsymbol{v}$, where λ is an arbitrary integer. It is easy to verify that the set of all such translations forms a group. We obtain the group of all translations which map the given linear pattern onto itself.

The parquet pattern shown in Figure 28 is also left invariant under certain translations provided we think of the pattern as being continued indefinitely. If two such translations are combined, then we obtain another mapping of the pattern onto

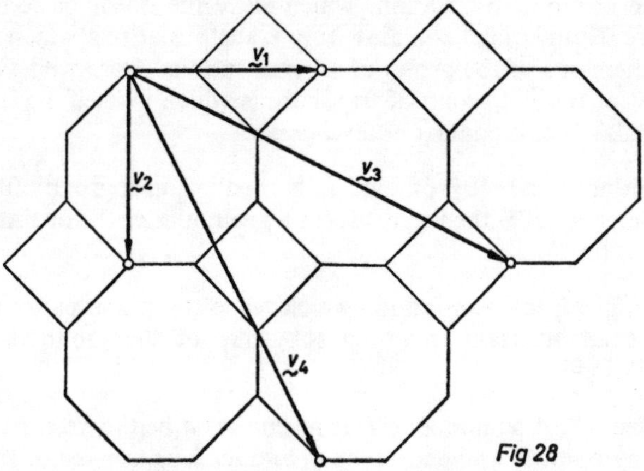

Fig 28

itself. The translations with vectors $\boldsymbol{v}_1$, $\boldsymbol{v}_2$, $\boldsymbol{v}_3$, $\boldsymbol{v}_4$ are examples of transformations which map the pattern onto itself. It is easily seen that all the translations with this property have vectors of the form

$$\boldsymbol{v} = \lambda \boldsymbol{v}_1 + \mu \boldsymbol{v}_2,$$

where λ and μ are integers, for example, $\boldsymbol{v}_3 = 2\boldsymbol{v}_1 + \boldsymbol{v}_2$, $\boldsymbol{v}_4 = \boldsymbol{v}_1 + 2\boldsymbol{v}_2$. These mappings again form a group; we call it the group of translations of the given plane pattern.

The idea of a group is not restricted to transformations. The definition of a group applies to other sets and operations. The study of such systems has developed into a special branch of mathematics—*group theory*. This theory provides a common framework for statements and methods concerning the most diverse fields of mathematics, provided that they are based on the same logical structure. Here one encounters mathematical thinking in its purest form.

In connection with the two groups of translations of patterns we should like to remark that groups of mappings of figures are sometimes used to characterize works of art, patterns and types of crystals.*

* See, for example, Coxeter, *Introduction to Geometry*, pp. 35, 278-9; Terpstra, *Some notes on the Mathematical Background of Repetitive Patterns*; Weyl, *Symmetry*.

The group of translations which leave the linear pattern of Figure 27 invariant contains only transformations which are also elements of the group of all translations. Here we have a subset of the full group of translations which is itself a group. One talks in this context of a *subgroup*.

Definition. A subset $\mathfrak{H}$ of a group $\mathfrak{G}$ is called a subgroup of $\mathfrak{G}$ if the elements of $\mathfrak{H}$ themselves form a group under the operation defined on $\mathfrak{G}$.

The group of translations which leave the plane pattern of Figure 28 invariant is also a subgroup of the group of all translations.

Problem 18. A square $ABCD$ is given. Let $\boldsymbol{a}$ be the vector with starting point D and end-point B, and let $\boldsymbol{b}$ be the vector from D to C. Find the image of the square under the translation with the vector $2\boldsymbol{a}+3\boldsymbol{b}$.

Problem 19. In a square $ABCD$ we define vectors $\boldsymbol{u} = \boldsymbol{AB}$ and $\boldsymbol{v} = \boldsymbol{AD}$. What is the figure formed by the images of this square if it is mapped by all the translations having vectors $\lambda\boldsymbol{u}+\mu\boldsymbol{v}$ where λ and μ are integers?

FURTHER EXAMPLES OF GROUPS

1. The group of integers under the operation of ordinary addition. The unit element is the number 0 and the inverse element to the number n is $-n$.
2. The group of even integers under the operation of addition. This is a subgroup of the previous example.
3. The group of rational numbers under the operation of addition. This group contains the two previous examples as subgroups.
4. The group of non-zero rational numbers under the operation of ordinary multiplication. Here the unit element is the number 1 and the inverse element to n is $1/n$.
5. The group of positive rational numbers under the operation of multiplication. This is a subgroup of the group of Example 4.

6. Let E be the symbol for an even number and O the symbol for an odd number. We take ordinary addition of numbers to be our operation of composition. Then we obtain the following rules of addition:

$E+E = E$ (even+even = even)
$E+O = O$ (even+odd = odd, independent of order)
$O+O = E$ (odd+odd = even).

This defines the operation of addition on the set $\{O,E\}$ and we can easily verify that these two elements form a group under the operation +. When a group contains only a finite number of elements, then we can describe it by means of a *group table* such as that below.

	+	Second element E	O
First element	E	E	O
	O	O	E

7. We divide all the integers into three classes according to the remainder left when they are divided by 3. We use the symbol R_0 for all integers divisible by 3, R_1 for those which leave the remainder 1 and R_2 for those integers which leave the remainder 2. There are no other integers. If, once more, we use addition as our operation, we obtain the following rules:

$$R_0+R_0 = R_0, \quad R_0+R_1 = R_1, \quad R_0+R_2 = R_2,$$
$$R_1+R_1 = R_2, \quad R_1+R_2 = R_0, \quad R_2+R_2 = R_1.$$

We can easily check that this system forms a group with three elements. The group table has the following form:

+	R_0	R_1	R_2
R_0	R_0	R_1	R_2
R_1	R_1	R_2	R_0
R_2	R_2	R_0	R_1

The three symbols R_0, R_1 and R_2 represent the *residue classes modulo* 3; this group is, therefore, called the group of residue classes modulo 3. Here R_0 is the unit element: the inverse element to R_1, for example, is R_2.

Problem 20. Check whether or not the following sets form groups under the given operations.

(a) The set $\mathfrak{G}$ of all positive fractions of the form $1/n$, under multiplication.

(b) The set $\mathfrak{R}$ of all residue classes modulo 5 other than the zero class (that is, the set $\mathfrak{R} = \{R_1, R_2, R_3, R_4\}$), under multiplication.

(c) The set $\mathfrak{R}$ of all residue classes modulo 6 other than the zero class, under multiplication.

(d) The set $\mathfrak{Y}$ of all integers, under subtraction.

(e) The set $\mathfrak{Y} = \{a+b\sqrt{2} : a,b \text{ rational; } a^2+b^2 \neq 0\}$, under multiplication.

(*f*) The set of all translations with vectors of the form $\lambda\boldsymbol{a}+\mu\boldsymbol{b}$ where $\boldsymbol{a}$ and $\boldsymbol{b}$ are given vectors and λ, μ are irrational numbers, under the operation of combination of transformations.

We conclude this first introduction to groups with an example of a non-associative operation. Let $\mathfrak{P}$ be the set of all points in the plane. With each pair of points A and B in $\mathfrak{P}$ we associate the point C which is the mid-point of the line segment AB. The reader should verify that the operation so defined is not associative. This example shows that one must not always assume the associativity of an operation.

4

ROTATIONS

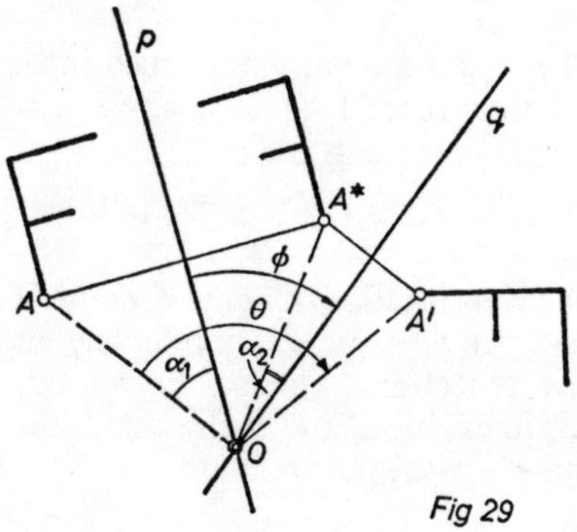

Fig 29

We now consider the product of two reflections M_p and M_q whose axes, p and q, intersect in the point O. The transformation $R = M_qM_p$ is a congruence which preserves orientation. Such congruences are known as *direct isometries*. The position of corresponding points A and $A' = R(A)$ is such that $OA = OA'$ and the angle

$$\theta = \angle AOA'$$

has a fixed value. We have in fact

$$\angle AOA' = 2\alpha_1 + 2\alpha_2 = 2\phi,$$

where ϕ is the angle between the axes of reflection p and q (see Figure 29).

The mapping R is called a *rotation* about O through the angle $\theta = 2\phi$. θ is known as the *angle of rotation* and O is the *centre of rotation*.

Problem 21. Verify the relation $\angle AOA' = 2\phi$ for different positions of A.

A rotation R is obviously determined once the centre and angle and direction of rotation are known. Angle and direction of rotation can be considered together as one quantity known as a *directed angle*. In this respect it is usual to consider angles to be positive if the direction of rotation is anticlockwise. Our statement concerning the product of M_p and M_q can now be written:

Theorem 6. If p and q are two lines which intersect at O, then M_qM_p is a rotation about O and the angle of rotation is twice the directed angle between p and q.

At the same time we can deduce the following theorem:

Theorem 7. A given rotation R about a point O and through a directed angle θ can be expressed in infinitely many ways as the product of two reflections. The axes of reflection p and q can be any pair of lines through O such that ϕ, the directed angle between p and q, satisfies the relation

$$\phi = \tfrac{1}{2}\theta.$$

Using Theorem 7 all rotations can be reduced to a product of reflections in exactly the same way as we found to be the case for translations. This will prove to be of value when we come to analyse isometries.

We can immediately deduce the following properties of rotations.

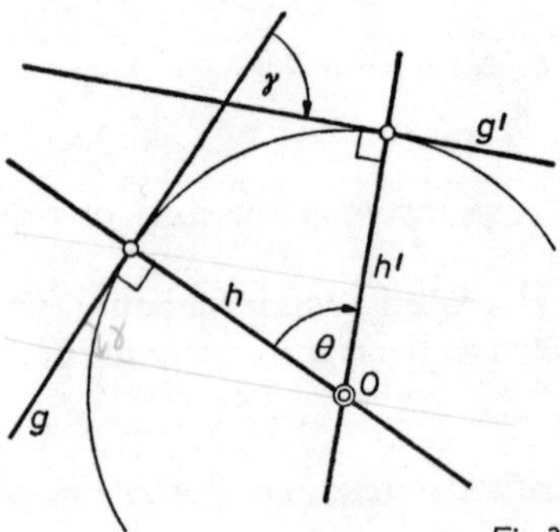

Fig 30

1. A rotation is a one-one mapping; the inverse mapping to $R(O,\theta)$ is the rotation $R^{-1}(O,-\theta)$.

2. Rotations are line-preserving transformations. The angle between a line g and its image g' is equal to the angle of rotation.

   This property is easily verified from Figure 30. The line h is the perpendicular to g through O and h' is its image. The angle between g and g' is $\gamma = \theta$.

3. A rotation has, in general, exactly one fixed point, namely the centre of rotation O. The exceptional cases arise when θ is a multiple of 360° in which case every point is a fixed point, that is, we have the identity transformation.

We shall now familiarize ourselves with this new type of transformation by making use of rotations to solve some construction problems.

Problem 22. Rotate a square $ABCD$ about a given point O through an angle $\theta = -60°$.

Problem 23. A point A and two lines b and d are given. Construct a square $ABCD$ such that B lies on b and D on d.*

We begin the solution of this problem by ignoring the condition on D. The remaining conditions determine an easily identifiable family of squares. If we draw the square with vertex X on b, then the opposite vertex X' is the image of X under a rotation about A through an angle $\theta = 90°$ (see Figure 31). If X moves on b, then X' moves on the image of b under this rotation, that is, on the line b'.

The problem has two solutions, since the rotation through $\theta = -90°$ will also provide a solution.

The solution to Problem 23 depended on the mapping of a geometric locus by a rotation. This same idea can be used to solve Problems 24 to 30.

* We assume that the vertices of the square are A, B, C, D in that order, cf. Problem 95.

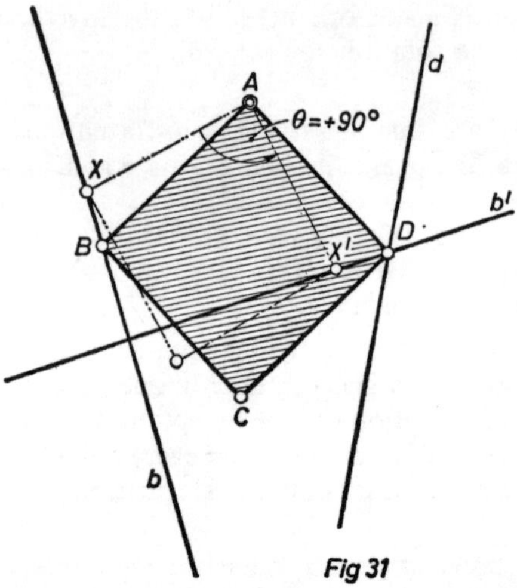

Fig 31

Problem 24. Construct an equilateral triangle which has one vertex at A and one vertex on each of the given lines b and c.

Problem 25. A point A and two lines b and c are given. Construct an isosceles triangle ABC such that B lies on b, C lies on c and $\angle ABC = \angle ACB = 75°$.

Problem 26. Given are a point A and two concentric circles Γ_1 and Γ_2. Construct an equilateral triangle with one vertex at A, the vertex B on Γ_1 and the vertex C on Γ_2.

Problem 27. Given are a point P and two circles Γ_1 and Γ_2. Find a point A on Γ_1 and a point B on Γ_2 such that P is the mid-point of AB.

Problem 28. Given are two circles Γ_1 and Γ_2 intersecting in the points P and Q. Construct a line through P which intersects the two circles in chords of equal length.

For the solution of Problems 27 and 28 we use rotations through 180°, that is, half-turns.

Problem 29. Given are three points A, B and C. Construct a square with centre A such that two adjoining sides (or their extensions) pass through B and C respectively.

Problem 30. P and Q are two points inside a circle Γ. Construct two chords of Γ of equal length, which intersect at an angle of 45° and such that one passes through P and the other through Q.

We now turn to another type of problem which can be solved by means of rotations. Now, however, the angle of rotation is not fixed; it depends upon how we draw the initial figure.

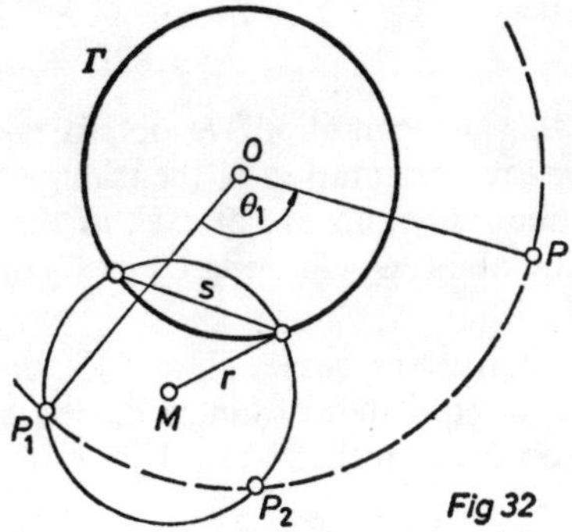

Fig 32

Problem 31. A circle Γ and a point P are given. Construct a second circle with a given radius r which passes through P and which has a common chord with Γ of length s.

We first ignore the condition that the circle should pass through P. Then there is a family of circles satisfying the remaining conditions and we can easily construct one of them; the circle with centre M (see Figure 32) is a representative of this family. To obtain a solution to the problem this circle must be rotated about O until it passes through P.

Problem 32. Given are a circle Γ and a line g. Construct a triangle with given sides which has the vertices A and B on Γ and the vertex C on g.

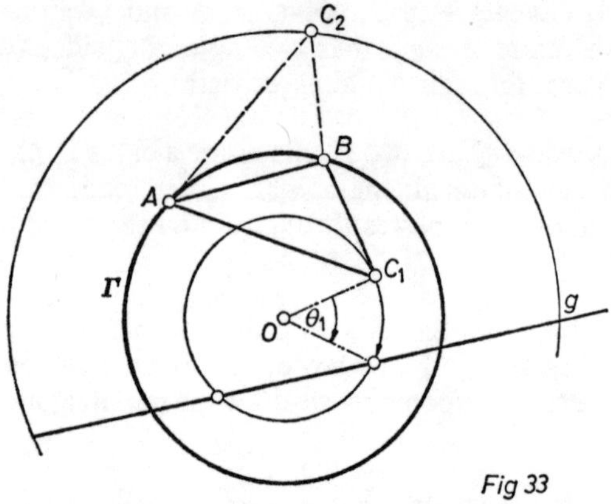

Fig 33

If we ignore the last condition we obtain two families of triangles, one for each orientation of the triangle. In Figure 33 we have drawn one representative of each of the two families. A suitable rotation about O will bring C_1 or C_2 onto the line g.

Problem 33. Two concentric circles Γ_1 and Γ_2, and a line g are given. Construct an equilateral triangle having sides of given length, d, and one vertex on each of Γ_1, Γ_2 and g.

We now continue our study of the theory of rotations by considering yet another type of problem.

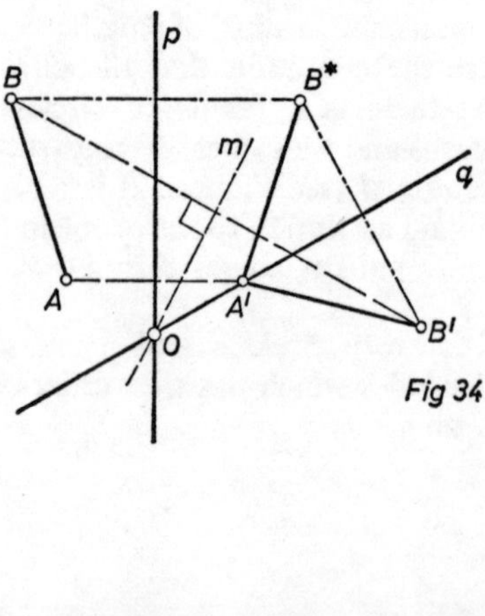

Fig 34

Problem 34. AB and $A'B'$ are two given directed line segments having the same length but not parallel. Show that there always exists a rotation R which maps A onto A' and B onto B'.

The problem is solved if we can find two reflections M_p and M_q such that $M_qM_p(A) = A'$, $M_qM_p(B) = B'$.

We take p to be the mediator of AA' and let B^* denote the image of B under M_p. If we now take q to be the mediator of B^*B', then M_p and M_q are the two reflections which satisfy our requirements. The centre of rotation O (the point of intersection of p and q) can also be found by a construction based on symmetry: O is the point of intersection of the mediators of AA' and BB' (see Figure 34). From this we can see that there is essentially only one rotation giving the required mapping (that is, there is only one rotation if we restrict the angle of rotation to lying between 0 and 360°).

Problem 35. What happens to the construction above if the line segments AB and $A'B'$ are
(a) symmetric with respect to a line,
(b) parallel but in an opposite sense?

Under the assumptions about AB and $A'B'$ which are listed in Problem 34 we can always find a rotation having the required properties. It seems reasonable, therefore, to see what happens in the exceptional case when the two directed line segments are parallel.

Assuming that AB and $A'B'$ are parallel directed line segments having equal lengths, then our construction leads to parallel axes of reflection. Hence, the transformation that

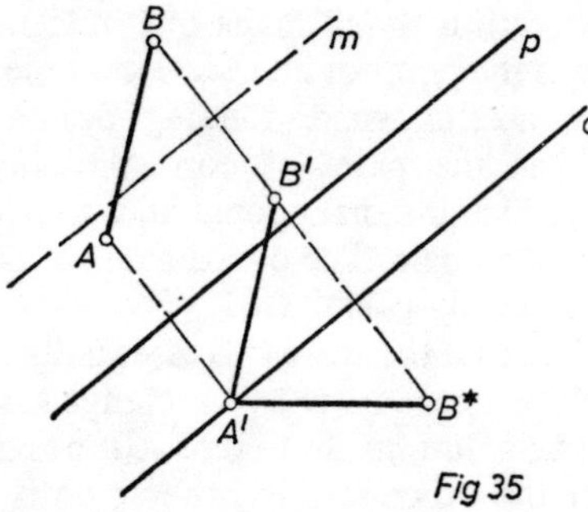

Fig 35

maps AB onto $A'B'$ is a translation. Translations can be considered as special cases of rotations, namely as rotations about a centre at an infinite distance through a zero angle.

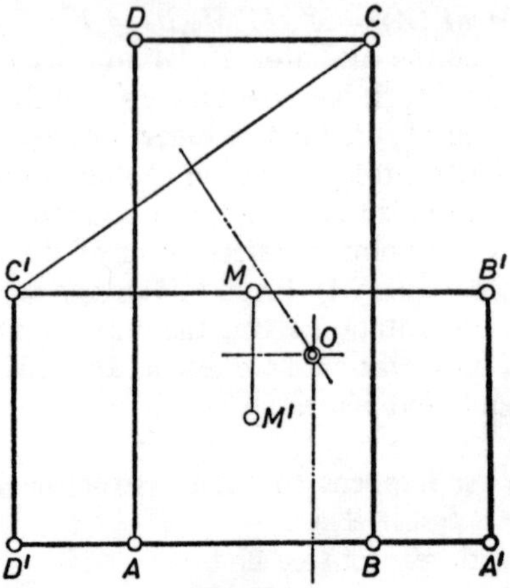

Fig 36

Problem 36. A rectangular table top of length 2 yd. and of width 1 yd. is to be fixed to the supporting frame in such a way that, by turning about an axis perpendicular to its plane, it can take the two positions indicated in Figure 36. Is this possible, and if so, about which point must the table top rotate?

Using the labelling of vertices indicated in Figure 36, the two rectangles $ABCD$ and $A'B'C'D'$ are congruent and have the same orientation. Since corresponding sides are not parallel, there must be a rotation which maps one onto the other. The centre of rotation is the point of intersection of the mediators of line segments connecting corresponding points. If we take A,A' and M,M' as the pairs of corresponding points, we obtain mediators which are orthogonal and, moreover, parallel to the sides of the rectangle. The coordinates of O with respect to $ABCD$ are then easily calculated.

It should be noted that there are two essentially different ways of associating the vertices of the two rectangles. Consequently the problem has two solutions. In Figure 36 the angle of rotation is $\theta = +90°$; for the other solution the angle is $\theta = -90°$.

COMBINATION OF ROTATIONS

We now consider the transformation resulting from the composition of two rotations. We shall see that, in general, we obtain another rotation and this will lead us to a new group of transformations.

We start with:

Problem 37. Map the square $ABCD$ by the rotation $R_1(O_1,\theta_1 = 60°)$ and then map its image by the rotation $R_2(O_2,\theta_2 = 90°)$. Show that the resultant mapping is again a rotation.

Figure 37 shows the various steps of the construction. The mapping R_2R_1 is obviously an isometry which preserves orientation, and it must again be a rotation. For, according to Problem 34, there is exactly one rotation which maps AD onto $A'D'$. This mapping, however, maps $ABCD$ onto $A'B'C'D'$. The centre of rotation O and the angle of rotation θ are easily constructed from AB and $A'B'$.

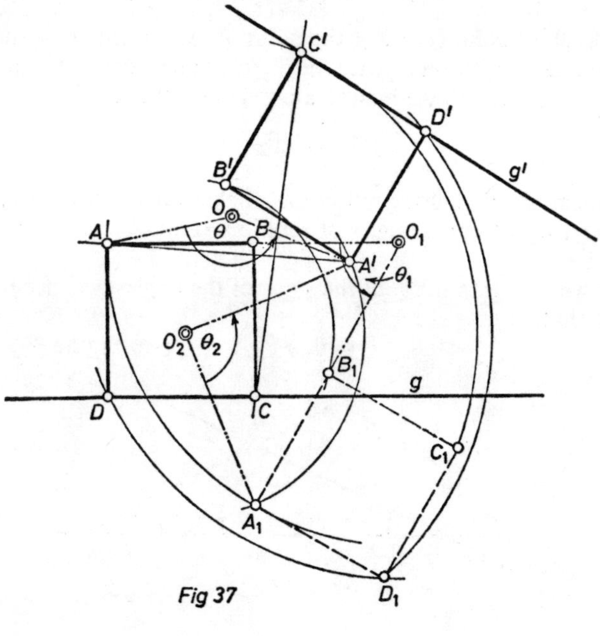

Fig 37

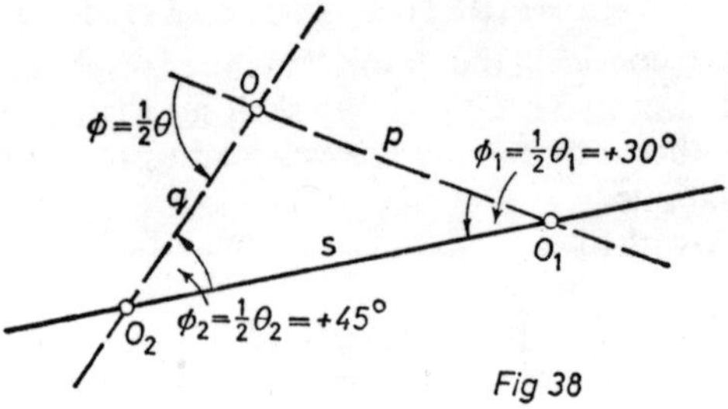

Fig 38

We analyse the product of two rotations further by considering a suitable decomposition of R_1 and R_2 into reflections. Let s be the line through the two centres of rotation, O_1 and O_2. By Theorem 7, we can decompose R_1 and R_2 in infinitely many ways into two reflections. We now select two lines p and q such that

$$R_1 = M_sM_p, \quad R_2 = M_qM_s.$$

Then

$$R = R_2R_1 = M_qM_sM_sM_p = M_qM_p.$$

The fixed point O of R is the point of intersection of p and q: the angle of rotation is twice the directed angle between p and q.

From Figure 38 we immediately deduce the relation

$$\theta = \theta_1+\theta_2.$$

Problem 38. Find, using reflections, the product of two rotations R_1 and R_2 when the angles of rotation θ_1 and θ_2 have different signs.

If we take into account the signs of the angles we once more find that

$$\theta = \theta_1+\theta_2 \qquad \text{(see Figure 39).}$$

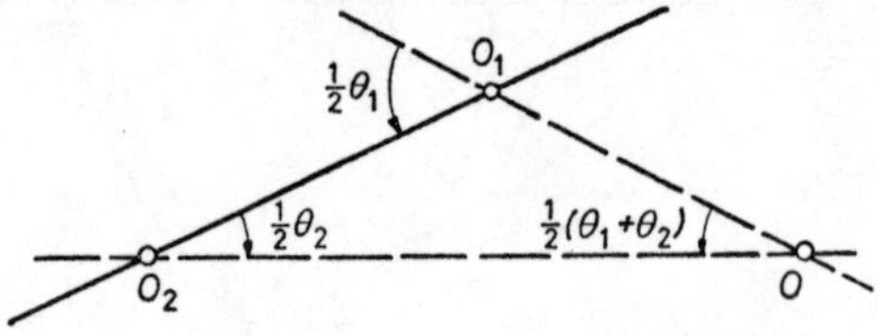

Fig 39

Theorem 8. When rotations are combined, the angles of rotation are added algebraically.

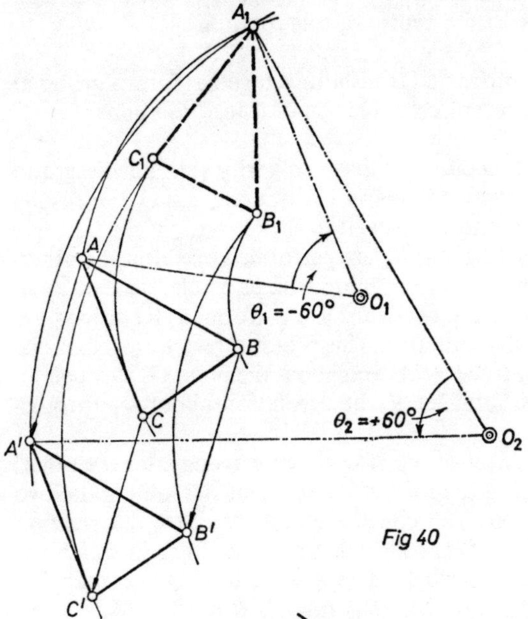

Fig 40

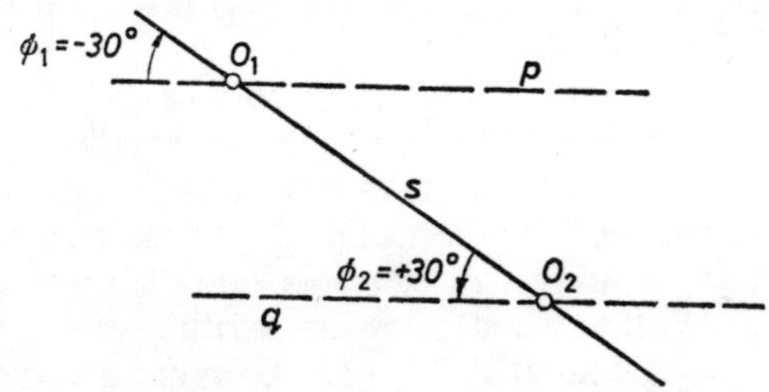

Fig. 41

If the two angles of rotation differ only in sign, that is, $\theta_1 + \theta_2 = 0$, then every line g is mapped onto a parallel line g' (see Figure 40).

Figure 41 illustrates how this case is analysed using reflections. We can see immediately that $R_2 R_1 = M_q M_p$ is a translation.

Problem 39. Given are a translation with vector $\boldsymbol{v}$ and a rotation about the point O through an angle $\theta = 60°$. The product of the two mappings, in the given order, is again a rotation through $\theta = 60°$. Construct the centre of this rotation.

Theorem 9. Rotations and translations together form a group $\mathfrak{B}$ under the operation of combination of transformations.

To prove this theorem we have to verify that all the group postulates are satisfied. This is easily done, using the results already obtained, and we leave it to the reader.

If two rotations R_1 and R_2 are performed one after the other, the final position of a given figure will, as a rule, depend upon the order in which the rotations are performed. Rotations are not, in general, commutative. This is best shown by an example.

Let us take R_1 to be a rotation about the point O_1 through an angle $\theta_1 = -60°$ and let R_2 be a rotation about O_2 through $\theta_2 = -90°$.

Consider the effect of the two mappings, one after the other, on a simple figure such as the line segment AB joining the two centres of rotation. The construction shows that the position of the final image of AB depends upon the order in which the two rotations are performed (see Figure 42). The mapping R_2R_1 (that is, first R_1 then R_2) maps AB onto $A_1'B_1'$; R_1R_2 maps AB onto $A_2'B_2'$.

The angle of rotation in both cases is $\theta_1+\theta_2$. Consequently the two image line segments are parallel.

The group of all translations and rotations, therefore, differs essentially from the group of all translations since the product of two of the group elements now depends upon the order in which the two elements are written. We say that the group is non-commutative. We note, however, that there are certain pairs of mappings in the group which do commute. For example, the product of two rotations about the same point is independent of the order in which the rotations are performed. However, the commutative law no longer holds in general.

Problem 40. R_1 and R_2 are two rotations. Construct the centres of R_2R_1 and R_1R_2 using suitable decompositions of R_1 and R_2 into products of reflections.

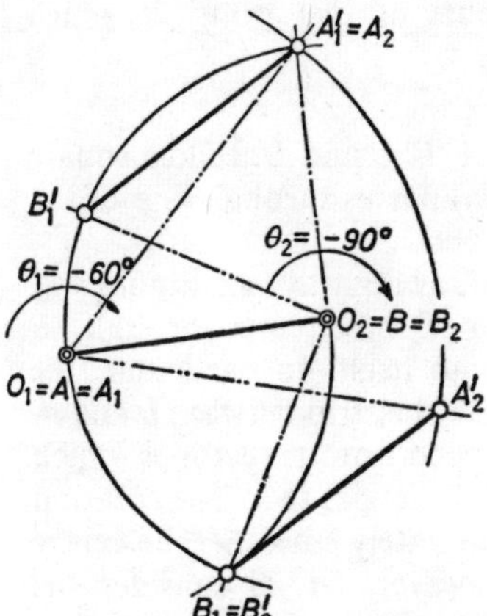

Fig 42

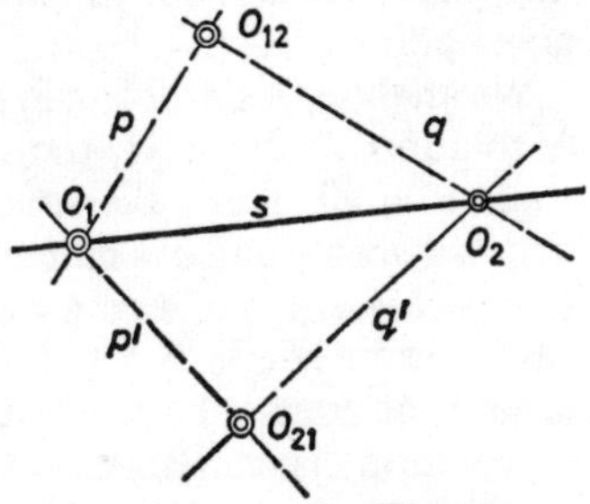

Fig. 43

Let s be the line between the two centres, we can then use the following decomposition which is indicated in Figure 43:

$$R_1 = M_s M_p = M_{p'} M_s, \quad R_2 = M_q M_s = M_s M_{q'}$$

We obtain

$$R_2 R_1 = M_q M_p, \quad R_1 R_2 = M_{p'} M_{q'}.$$

The fixed points of the two rotations $R_2 R_1$ and $R_1 R_2$ are, therefore, symmetrically placed with respect to the line s.

Problem 41. Given are two rotations R_1 and R_2. Find those points which are mapped onto the same image point under R_1 and R_2.

Hint: a point with this property is a fixed point under $R_2^{-1} R_1$.

Problem 42. If R_1 and R_2 are two arbitrary rotations, show that the centres of R_1, $R_2 R_1$ and $R_2^{-1} R_1$ are collinear.

Problem 43. A, B and C are the vertices of a triangle (described in a clockwise direction), and α, β, γ are the angles at A, B and C respectively. Show that the three rotations $R_1(A, 2\alpha)$, $R_2(B, 2\beta)$, $R_3(C, 2\gamma)$ satisfy the relation

$$R_3 R_2 R_1 = \text{I}.$$

Problem 44. Give pairs of elements of the group 𝔅 which commute with each other.

Problem 45. Given are four points *A*, *B*, *C* and *D*. Find a square such that each side (or its extension) passes through one of the given points.

We analyse this problem in the following way (see Figure 44). A rotation *R* about *M*, the centre of the square, through an angle $\theta = 90°$ maps the square onto itself. In particular, the strip between *a* and *c* is mapped onto the strip between *b* and *d*. The vector $\boldsymbol{u}$ (from *A* to *C*) is mapped onto a vector $\boldsymbol{w}$ which has the same length as $\boldsymbol{u}$ and is at right-angles to $\boldsymbol{u}$. The rotation cannot, of course, be realized immediately since *M*, the centre of rotation, is still unknown. However, let us consider the product of this rotation and a translation *T* with vector $\boldsymbol{t}$. This maps C' onto $C^* = D$ and maps A' onto A^*. The vector $\boldsymbol{w}$ is not changed since vectors are invariant under translations—it is only moved to another position.

The mapping *TR* can now be constructed. It maps $\boldsymbol{u}$ onto the

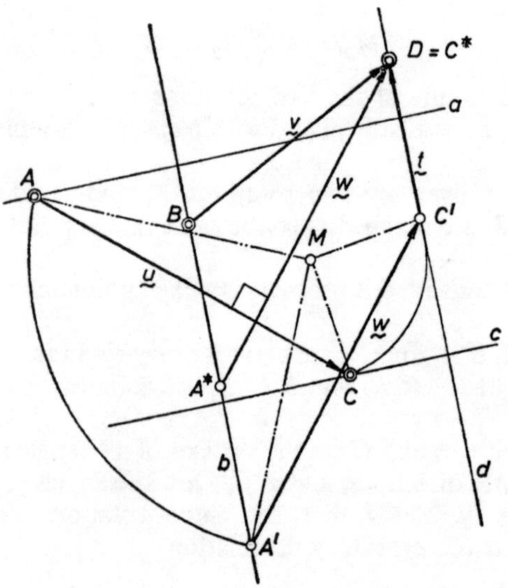

Fig.44

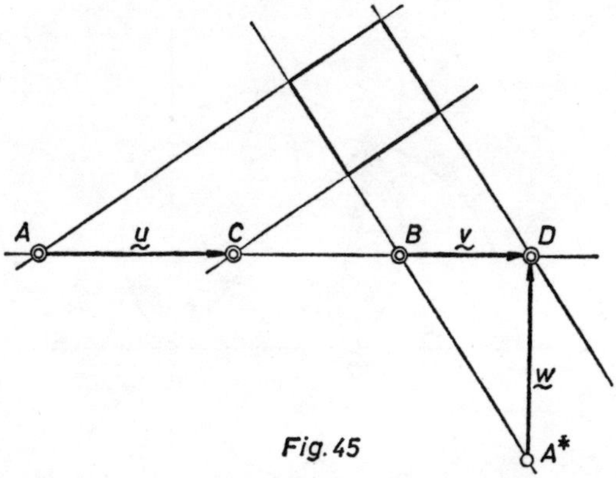

Fig. 45

vector $\boldsymbol{w}$ which has the above mentioned properties and, moreover, has its end-point at D. We can now construct this vector without any difficulty. But once we have constructed $\boldsymbol{w}$ we have found A^*, that is, a second point on the side of the square through B. This enables us to draw the side b and the remaining sides of the square can then be readily constructed.

We leave it to the reader to check that this problem has six different solutions. Figure 45 shows how the square is constructed for a special disposition of the points A, B, C, D.

Problem 46. Given are three points A, B, C. Construct a square which has A as a vertex and such that one of its two sides not passing through A passes through B and the other through C.

This is a special case of Problem 45. Here two of the given points coincide.

In the solution of Problem 45 we used a rotation TR which mapped the strip between the lines a and c onto the strip bounded by b and d. In particular, a was mapped onto b and c onto d. There are infinitely many rotations through an angle $\theta = 90°$ which do this. We now consider the problem of finding the geometrical locus of the centres of such rotations.

Problem 47. Given are two perpendicular lines g and g' which intersect at the point S. Find the geometric locus of the centres of all rotations which map g onto g' (see Figure 46).

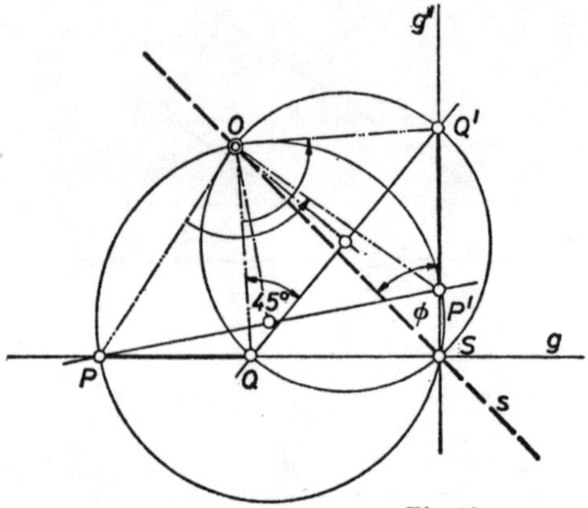

Fig. 46

Every rotation mapping g onto g' maps a line segment PQ on g onto a line segment $P'Q'$, of the same length, on g'. In drawing P' and Q' we have to take into account the direction of rotation. The rotation is completely determined by the choice of such a pair of line segments. The centre of rotation, O, is the intersection of the mediators of PP' and QQ'. The fact that $\theta = 90°$ means that O lies on the circles having PP' and QQ' as diameters. These two circles, moreover, pass through S. Hence, we have

$$\angle OSQ' = \angle OQQ' = 45°.$$

The geometric locus of the centres of all the rotations through an angle $\theta = 90°$ which map g onto g' is, therefore, one line bisecting the angle between g and g'.

There are also rotations with $\theta = -90°$ which map g onto g'; the geometric locus of their centres is the other bisector.

Problem 48. This is a generalization of Problem 47. Given are two lines g and g' which now meet at an arbitrary angle ψ. Find the geometric locus of the centres of all the rotations mapping g onto g'.

Problem 49. Show that the set of all translations and half-turns forms a subgroup $\mathfrak{B}'$ of $\mathfrak{B}$.

The proof of this should present no particular difficulty.

We denote the fact that the elements of $\mathfrak{B}'$ are also elements of $\mathfrak{B}$ by writing $\mathfrak{B}' \subset \mathfrak{B}$.

If we again denote the set of all translations by $\mathfrak{T}$, then we have the following chain of inclusions:

$$\mathfrak{T} \subset \mathfrak{B}' \subset \mathfrak{B}.$$

We conclude our study of the group $\mathfrak{B}'$ by considering some typical problems.

Problem 50. Show that the product of an odd number of half-turns is always a half-turn.

Hint: use the fact that the product of two half-turns is a translation.

Problem 51. Given five points P, Q, R, S, T, construct a pentagon having these points as the mid-points of its sides.

The vertices of the pentagon have been denoted by F, F_1, F_2, F_3, F_4 (see Figure 47). F is mapped onto itself by the following chain of half-turns:

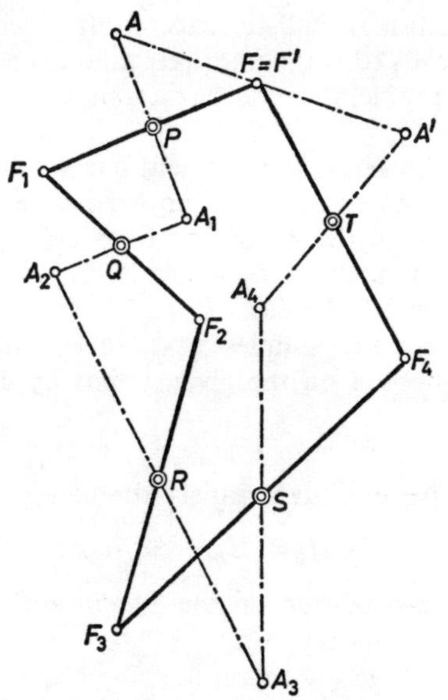

Fig. 47

$$F \xrightarrow[H_P]{} F_1 \xrightarrow[H_Q]{} F_2 \xrightarrow[H_R]{} F_3 \xrightarrow[H_S]{} F_4 \xrightarrow[H_T]{} F' = F.$$

F is, therefore, a fixed point of the mapping

$$\Omega = H_T H_S H_R H_Q H_P.$$

From Problem 50, Ω is a half-turn. Its centre, F, can be constructed by mapping any point A in the plane by Ω. F is then the mid-point of AA'.

The fixed point F can also be obtained without mapping a figure (cf. Problem 15 and Figure 22).

We note that this problem always has a solution.

Problem 52. Construct an n-sided polygon, when the mid-points M_i ($i = 1, \ldots, n$) of all the sides are given.

This is a generalization of Problem 51. Let us denote the half-turn about M_i by H_i and consider

$$\Omega = H_n H_{n-1} \ldots H_2 H_1.$$

Ω is a translation or half-turn according to whether n is even or odd. This leads to two completely different solutions. If n is odd, then the problem always has a unique solution just as in the case $n = 5$.

For even n, however, the problem has a solution only if Ω is the identity; otherwise Ω has no fixed point. But if $\Omega = I$, then every point in the plane is a fixed point; hence, in this case there are infinitely many n-sided polygons with the given points as mid-points of sides.

Consider in the two simplest cases, $n = 4$ and $n = 6$, what condition is imposed on the given points by demanding that $\Omega = I$.

Problem 53. Five half-turns satisfy the relation

$$H_E H_D H_C H_B H_A = H_C.$$

What geometric condition on the disposition of the points is characterized by this relation?

We first rearrange the relation:

$$H_E H_D H_C H_B H_A = H_C \Leftrightarrow H_C H_E H_D H_C H_B H_A = I.$$

If we now apply Theorem 4 to the three left-hand factors we obtain:

$$H_D H_E H_C H_C H_B H_A = I \Leftrightarrow H_D H_E H_B H_A = I.$$

This last relation holds if, and only if, A, B, E, D are the vertices of a parallelogram (which may be collapsed onto a line).

The position of the point C, therefore, is arbitrary and A, B, E, D are the vertices of a parallelogram.

Problem 54. Given are two lines a, b and the three points P, Q and R. Construct a path consisting of three line segments which has the properties:
(a) the path starts on a and ends on b,
(b) P, Q and R are the mid-points of the three segments.

5

THE GROUP OF ISOMETRIES

We now study the set $\mathfrak{K}$ of all isometries, that is, of all transformations which preserve congruence. $\mathfrak{K}$ is the set of all finite products of reflections:

$$\Omega = M_{f_n} M_{f_{n-1}} \dots M_{f_2} M_{f_1}.$$

Ω is a *direct* (orientation preserving) or an *opposite* (orientation reversing) isometry according to whether n is even or odd.

Problem 55. Show that the set $\mathfrak{K}$ under the operation of combination of transformations is a group.

$\mathfrak{K}$ is called the *group of plane isometries.*

We have called figures *congruent* if they can be mapped onto each other by mappings in the group $\mathfrak{K}$. This notion of congruence has the following remarkable properties.

1. Every figure is congruent to itself: $F_1 \cong F_1$ (*property of reflexivity*).

2. If F_1 is congruent to F_2, then F_2 is congruent to F_1 and vice-versa:

$$F_1 \cong F_2 \Leftrightarrow F_2 \cong F_1 \text{ (\textit{property of symmetry})}.$$

3. If F_1 is congruent to F_2 and F_2 is congruent to F_3, then F_1 is congruent to F_3:

$$F_1 \cong F_2 \text{ and } F_2 \cong F_3 \Rightarrow F_1 \cong F_3 \text{ (\textit{property of transitivity})}.$$

Definition. The properties of reflexivity, symmetry and transitivity characterize an *equivalence relation.*

Equivalent figures form what is known as an *equivalence class*.

As examples of equivalence classes with respect to congruence, we have:

the set of all squares with sides of a given length d;

the set of all pairs of points a distance d apart;

the set of all right-angled triangles with sides 3 in., 4 in., 5 in.

Problem 56. Show that the concept of parallelism defined on p. 28 is an equivalence relation.

We now want to give a complete description of the mappings in $\mathfrak{K}$. We first consider the direct isometries and show:

Theorem 10. A direct isometry with two distinct fixed points is necessarily the identity transformation I.

Assume that Φ has the two fixed points F_1 and F_2 (see Figure 48). Then the line f joining F_1 to F_2 is obviously a pointwise fixed line. Now let P be an arbitrary point in the plane and h be the perpendicular from P to f. Since the right-angle between f and h is left unchanged by the mapping Φ, we conclude that h is also a fixed line. There are now two possibilities to consider: either $P' = P$ or P' and P are symmetrically placed with respect to f. This latter possibility is ruled out since Φ is an orientation preserving isometry. Hence, all points of the plane are fixed points, that is, $\Phi = I$.

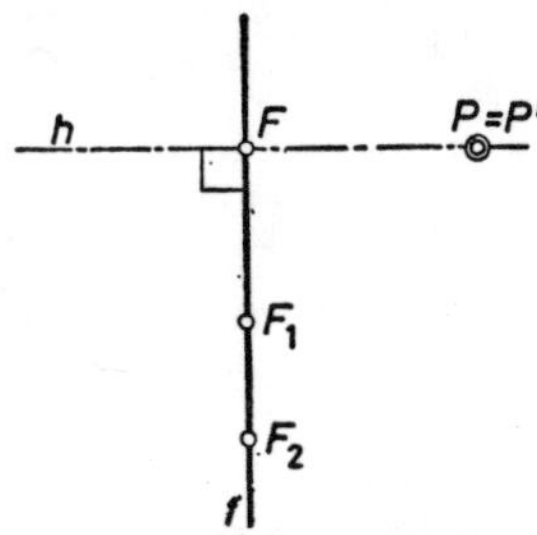

Fig. 48

Now take an arbitrary direct isometry Ω, that is, a product of an even number of reflections. Let $A'B'$ be the image under Ω of a line segment AB. Problem 34 tells us that there are two reflections M_p and M_q such that M_qM_p maps AB onto $A'B'$ (see Figure 34). Hence, $M_pM_q\Omega$ is a direct isometry with the two fixed points A and B and is, therefore, the identity. However,

$$M_p M_q \Omega = I \Leftrightarrow \Omega = M_q M_p.$$

We state this as:

Theorem 11. Every direct isometry can be expressed as the product of two reflections and is therefore a translation or a rotation. The direct isometries are the elements of $\mathfrak{B}$. $\mathfrak{B}$ is known as the *group of direct isometries.*

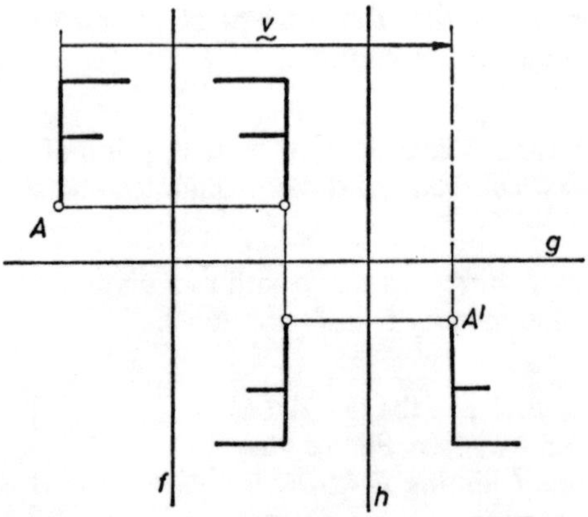

Fig. 49

Now we turn to the opposite isometries. We start with a simple example, the mapping

$$\Phi = M_h M_g M_f,$$

where f and h are perpendiculars to g (see Figure 49).

Remembering that the order in which two reflections are performed can be interchanged if their axes are orthogonal, we deduce that

$$\Phi = M_h M_g M_f = M_h M_f M_g = M_g M_h M_f.$$

But $M_h M_f = T$ is a translation; hence we can write

$$\Phi = T M_g = M_g T.$$

Our orientation reversing isometry is, therefore, the product of a reflection and a translation with a vector $\boldsymbol{v}$ parallel to the axis of reflection. We call this type of opposite isometry a *glide-reflection.* For $\mathbf{v} = 0$ this reduces to a reflection. Reflections are, therefore, special cases of glide-reflections.

Theorem 12. Every opposite isometry is a glide-reflection.

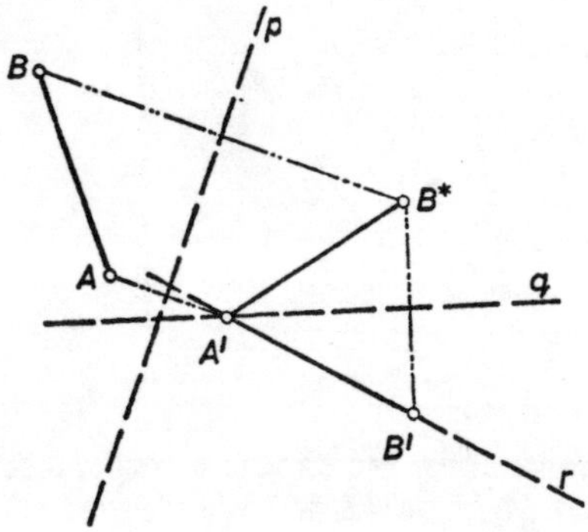

Fig. 50

In order to prove this surprising fact we consider an opposite isometry Ω. Let $A'B'$ be the image of a line segment AB under Ω (see Figure 50).

According to Problem 34, we can find two lines p and q such that M_qM_p also maps AB onto $A'B'$. We now introduce the line r which joins A' and B'. We easily verify that $M_pM_qM_r\Omega$ is a direct isometry with the two fixed points A and B. From Theorem 10, it must be the identity I:

$$M_pM_qM_r\Omega = I \Leftrightarrow \Omega = M_rM_qM_p.$$

Hence, Ω can be written as a product of three reflections. It remains to show that every product of three reflections is a glide-reflection.

We have to distinguish between the two cases:

(a) p, q, r are parallel. In this situation it is easy to see that Ω can be reduced to a single reflection.

(b) p and r are not both parallel to q. Let us assume that q and r intersect in a point R. Then M_rM_q represents a rotation which, according to Theorem 7, can also be written as a product of

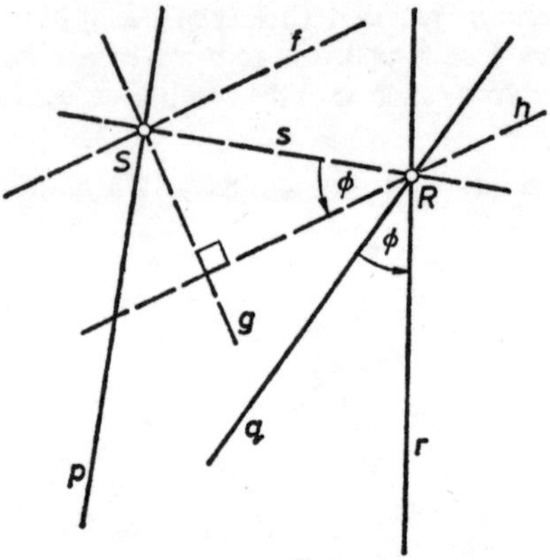

Fig. 51

two different reflections. We choose s perpendicular to p and a line h such that $M_r M_q = M_h M_s$. We then have

$$\Omega = M_r M_q M_p = M_h M_s M_p = M_h H_S.$$

Now split the half-turn H_S into two reflections M_f and M_g, where f is parallel to, and g perpendicular to, h. This gives us a representation

$$\Omega = M_h H_S = M_h M_g M_f,$$

which can immediately be seen to be a glide-reflection with the axis g.

Now we can state:

Theorem 13. The group $\mathfrak{K}$ contains only four types of mappings, namely translations, rotations, reflections and glide-reflections.

Note that Theorem 13 also tells us that every mapping Ω of $\mathfrak{K}$ can be represented as a product of at most three reflections.

Problem 57. What type of glide-reflection is $\Omega = M_r M_q M_p$, if:
(a) p, q, r form an equilateral triangle;
(b) p, q, r form a right-angled triangle;
(c) p, q, r all pass through the point S?

It is to be noted that a glide-reflection with a fixed point is a reflection.

Problem 58. Show that, if the lines p, q and r form a triangle, then the axis of the glide-reflection $\Omega = M_r M_q M_p$ passes through two of the feet of the altitudes of the triangle.

Problem 59. Two congruent line segments AB and $A'B'$ are given. Construct the axis, g, and the vector, $\boldsymbol{v}$, of the glide-reflection which maps A onto A' and B onto B'.

One way of finding g and $\boldsymbol{v}$ is to express Ω as a product of three reflections as in Figure 50, and to reduce this to another triple product as in Figure 49. There is, however, a simpler way. If we choose the line f in the representation $\Omega = M_h M_g M_f = H_H M_f$, given in Figure 49, to pass through A, then A is a fixed point of M_f. Hence A' is the image of A under H_H. We deduce that the mid-point of AA' must lie on the axis g (see Figure 52). Using this property we can immediately construct g from the two pairs of points A, A' and B, B'.

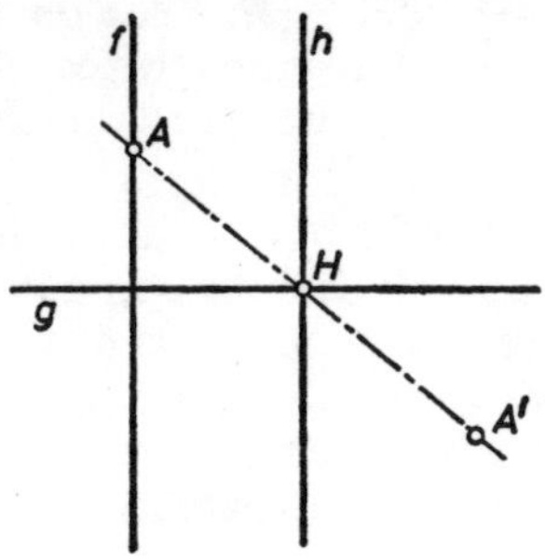

Fig. 52

Problem 60. Investigate the following isometries:

(a) $M_g H_S$, if S lies on g;

(b) $M_g H_S$, if S does not lie on g;

(c) $H_A M_f H_A$;

(d) $M_a H_F M_a$.

Discuss the decomposition of half-turns into suitable products of reflections.

Problem 61. Verify the following equivalence:

$$(M_g H_S)^2 = I \Leftrightarrow S \text{ lies on } g.$$

THE ROLE OF REFLECTIONS AND HALF-TURNS IN THE GROUP $\mathfrak{K}$

The group $\mathfrak{K}$ contains two types of involutions: reflections and half-turns. These simple mappings bear a close relation to the basic elements of plane geometry: lines and points. Corresponding to every point and every line there is a unique transformation. A geometric relation of incidence between points and lines corresponds to a group relation between the corresponding transformations. For example in Problem 61 we found the equivalence

1. $M_g H_S M_g H_S = I \Leftrightarrow S$ lies on g.

Another example of equivalent statements is

2. $H_K H_H H_G H_F = I \Leftrightarrow \begin{cases} F, G, H, K \text{ are the vertices of a parallelogram (which may be collapsed} \\ \text{onto a line). (See Figure 22.)} \end{cases}$

We now wish to look for other equivalences of this kind.

$(M_r M_q M_p)^2 = I$ means that the opposite isometry $M_r M_q M_p$ is a reflection M_f; hence $M_q M_p = M_r M_f$. The mapping which is here described in two ways is either a rotation or a translation. In the first case p, q and r all pass through a point O, in the second case the three lines are parallel. In either case p, q, r lie in a pencil of lines.

We have, therefore, the equivalence

3. $(M_r M_q M_p)^2 = I \Leftrightarrow p, q, r$ belong to a pencil.

If F is the mid-point of the line segment AB, then $H_F H_A$ and $H_B H_F$ both represent the same translation. Hence

4. $H_F H_B H_F H_A = I \Leftrightarrow F$ is the mid-point of AB.

Problem 62. Verify the following equivalences:

5. $M_f H_B M_f H_A = I \Leftrightarrow f$ is the mediator of AB;

6. $M_f M_b M_f M_a = I \Leftrightarrow f$ is a bisector (or mid-parallel) of a and b;

7. $\left.\begin{matrix}(H_F H_B)^n (H_F H_A)^m = I \\ (m, n \text{ positive integers})\end{matrix}\right\} \Leftrightarrow \left\{\begin{matrix}F \text{ divides the segment } AB \text{ in-} \\ \text{ternally in the ratio } n{:}m;\end{matrix}\right.$

8. $\left.\begin{matrix}(H_B H_F)^n (H_F H_A)^m = I \\ (m, n \text{ positive integers})\end{matrix}\right\} \Leftrightarrow \left\{\begin{matrix}F \text{ divides the segment } AB \text{ ex-} \\ \text{ternally in the ratio } n{:}m;\end{matrix}\right.$

9. $H_B M_f H_B H_A M_f H_A = I \Leftrightarrow f$ is parallel to the line AB;

10. $(H_B M_f H_A)^2 = I \Leftrightarrow f$ is perpendicular to the line AB;

11. $H_S H_C H_S H_B H_S H_A = I \Leftrightarrow S$ is the centroid of the triangle ABC.

All the group relations on the left-hand side have the same structure; they are products of transformations representing the identity. We shall call such products cycles of reflections and half-turns.

These equivalences enable us to translate geometric relations concerning position into algebraic language, and to translate back. This idea leads to a new method of proof for geometric theorems. The following problem serves to introduce this method.

Problem 63. Show that a line through the mid-points of two sides of a triangle is parallel to the third side.

We begin the proof by translating the given geometric relations of position into algebraic relations:

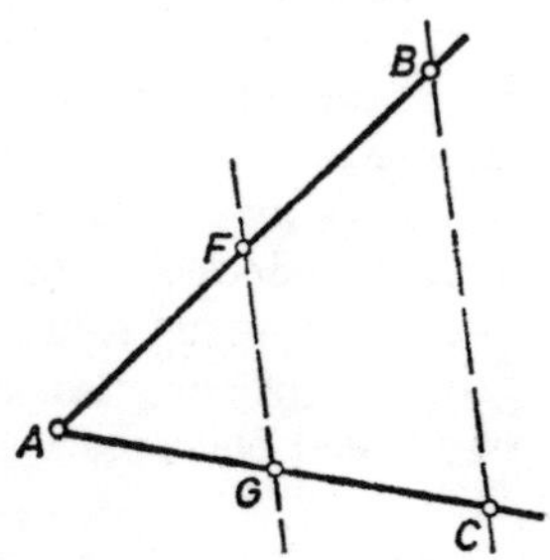

Fig. 53

F is the mid-point of $AB \Leftrightarrow H_F H_B H_F H_A = I$;
G is the mid-point of $AC \Leftrightarrow H_G H_C H_G H_A = I$.

From these we deduce

$$\begin{aligned} H_C H_B &= H_G H_A H_G H_F H_A H_F \\ &= H_G H_F H_G H_A H_A H_F \quad \text{(using Theorem 4)} \\ &= (H_G H_F)^2. \end{aligned}$$

The result $H_C H_B = (H_G H_F)^2$ means that $BC = 2FG$. We have proved even more than was required, for we have also shown that the segment FG is half as long as BC.*

Here we have proved a theorem in geometry by means of algebraic manipulations with half-turns. This method can be extended and other groups of mappings can be used to provide proofs of geometric theorems.

Problem 64. Prove, using reflections and half-turns, that the mediators of the sides of a triangle are concurrent.

We restrict ourselves here to giving an outline of the solution. Let f and g be the mediators of the sides AB and AC, and let a be the line joining D, the point of intersection of f and g, to the vertex A. Then $M_g M_a M_f$ is obviously a reflection in a line. It is then easy to show that the axis of this reflection is the third mediator.

We conclude our study of the group of isometries with the following remarks. It is now possible, using the knowledge of mappings and groups which we have gained so far, to define the somewhat vague idea of geometry more exactly. Geometry, in the sense of Felix Klein, is a study of those quantities and properties of figures which are left invariant under all the mappings of a group; it is the study of invariants of a certain group of mappings. For every group of mappings we can, therefore, develop a particular geometry.

Corresponding to the group $\mathfrak{K}$ of isometries is the so-called geometry of congruences, which formed the main part of the traditional elementary geometry course.

* It should be noted that this is a special case of the theorem that rays through a given point are divided by parallel lines in equal ratios. No assumptions about continuity are required for our proof of this special case.

6

THE GROUP OF TRANSFORMATIONS MAPPING A SQUARE ONTO ITSELF

The group $\mathfrak{K}$ contains translations, rotations, reflections and glide-reflections.

We now wish to enumerate all the isometries which map a square *ABCD* onto itself. Obviously, no translation or glide-reflection can map the square onto itself, and so we need only consider rotations and reflections. It is easy to see that the square is mapped onto itself by the eight isometries shown in Figure 54.

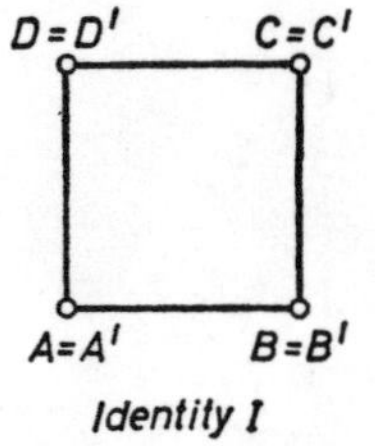

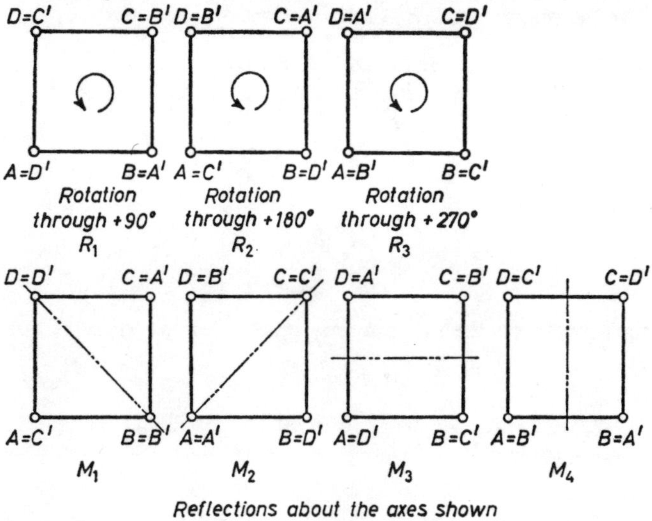

Fig. 54

There are no other isometries which leave the square invariant and so the product of any two of these mappings must again be one of the eight. For the same reason, the inverse of each of these mappings must also belong to this set of eight. Therefore, we have a group which has only a finite number of elements. We have already met finite groups defined by means of numbers and so it should not surprise us to find that finite groups also occur in transformation geometry.

Before discussing this group further we wish to know how we can find the product of any two of its elements. This will considerably simplify the working out of the group table. The mapping R_2, for example, maps A onto C, B onto D, C onto A and D onto B. We express this by writing

$$R_2 = \begin{Bmatrix} A & B & C & D \\ C & D & A & B \end{Bmatrix}:$$

similarly,

$$M_3 = \begin{Bmatrix} A & B & C & D \\ D & C & B & A \end{Bmatrix}.$$

For the mapping M_3R_2 (first R_2, then M_3) we have

$$\begin{array}{ccccc} & A & B & C & D \\ R_2 & \downarrow & \downarrow & \downarrow & \downarrow \\ & C & D & A & B \\ M_3 & \downarrow & \downarrow & \downarrow & \downarrow \\ & B & A & D & C \end{array}$$

that is,

$$M_3R_2 = \begin{Bmatrix} A & B & C & D \\ B & A & D & C \end{Bmatrix}.$$

This, however, is the mapping M_4. Hence, we get the relation

$$M_3R_2 = M_4.$$

If, in this way, we work out all the products we get the following table.*

* Note that we find the product M_3R_2 by looking in the row labelled M_3 and the column headed R_2.

	I	R_1	R_2	R_3	M_1	M_2	M_3	M_4
I	I	R_1	R_2	R_3	M_1	M_2	M_3	M_4
R_1	R_1	R_2	R_3	I	M_3	M_4	M_2	M_1
R_2	R_2	R_3	I	R_1	M_2	M_1	M_4	M_3
R_3	R_3	I	R_1	R_2	M_4	M_3	M_1	M_2
M_1	M_1	M_4	M_2	M_3	I	R_2	R_3	R_1
M_2	M_2	M_3	M_1	M_4	R_2	I	R_1	R_3
M_3	M_3	M_1	M_4	M_2	R_1	R_3	I	R_2
M_4	M_4	M_2	M_3	M_1	R_3	R_1	R_2	I

This group table has the following remarkable properties.

In every row and every column, every element (mapping) occurs exactly once. *This is a property of all group tables.*

I and the elements R_1, R_2 and R_3 form a group by themselves (see the top left-hand quarter square of the group table). That is, our group of eight elements contains a subgroup of four elements consisting of those mappings which preserve the orientation of the square. Here again we learn a general fact about groups of mappings: *if we demand additional invariants, then the group is restricted to a subgroup.*

The group is non-commutative. It does contain pairs of elements which commute, but we have, for example,

$$M_2R_3 = M_4 \text{ and } R_3M_2 = M_3.$$

Since group multiplication is associative, we can work out higher products. This corresponds geometrically to the product of more than two mappings. For example.

$$\begin{aligned} M_1R_3M_2R_3M_4 &= (M_1R_3)M_2(R_3M_4) \\ &= M_3(M_2M_2) \\ &= M_3I \\ &= M_3. \end{aligned}$$

Every other way of working out this product leads to this same result. This is the content of the associative law, that is, the group postulate IV.

Hence, we get the same result by the following bracketings of the factors:

$$M_1R_3M_2R_3M_4 = (M_1R_3)(M_2R_3)M_4 = (M_3M_4)M_4 = R_2M_4 = M_3;$$

$$M_1R_3M_2R_3M_4 = M_1R_3M_2(R_3M_4) = M_1R_3(M_2M_2) = M_1R_3 = M_3.$$

We stress once more that the operation of combining transformations is always associative.

We shall now demonstrate a general theorem of group theory by considering our finite group. Denote our group of isometries by $\mathfrak{G}_8$. We can see immediately that the two elements I and R_2 form a subgroup $\mathfrak{H}_2$. If we now multiply both elements of $\mathfrak{H}_2$ by an element of $\mathfrak{G}_8$ not belonging to $\mathfrak{H}_2$—say by M_1—we obtain the set of elements

$$M_1\mathfrak{H}_2 = \{M_1I, M_1R_2\} = \{M_1, M_2\}.$$

These are two elements of $\mathfrak{G}_8$ not belonging to $\mathfrak{H}_2$. If we take another element of $\mathfrak{G}_8$ which has not occurred so far, for example, M_3, we obtain in the same way

$$M_3\mathfrak{H}_2 = \{M_3I, M_3R_2\} = \{M_3, M_4\}.$$

If we repeat this process with one of the remaining elements of $\mathfrak{G}_8$, for example, R_1, we obtain

$$R_1\mathfrak{H}_2 = \{R_1I, R_1R_2\} = \{R_1, R_3\}.$$

Now we have a complete partitioning of the elements of $\mathfrak{G}_8$ based on the subgroup $\mathfrak{H}_2$. We may speak of it as a decomposition of $\mathfrak{G}_8$ with respect to $\mathfrak{H}_2$, and we write

$$\mathfrak{G}_2 = \mathfrak{H}_2+\{M_1, M_2\}+\{M_3, M_4\}+\{R_1, R_3\}.$$

The elements of $\mathfrak{G}_8$ by which we 'multiplied' $\mathfrak{H}_2$ are not uniquely determined. We remark, however, without proof that the decomposition of $\mathfrak{G}_8$ with respect to $\mathfrak{H}_2$ is, nevertheless, unique; we always obtain the same four classes. The essential fact is that $\mathfrak{G}_8$ can be divided into a number of classes which all contain the same number of elements, namely the same number of elements as are contained in $\mathfrak{H}_2$. This is true for every subgroup $\mathfrak{H}$ of a finite group $\mathfrak{G}$. After a finite number of steps the process of splitting into classes terminates and we always obtain a number of classes with the same number of elements in each of them. So we have verified in a special case the general statement:

If a finite group $\mathfrak{G}$ has a subgroup $\mathfrak{H}$, then the number of elements in $\mathfrak{H}$ is always a divisor of the number of elements in $\mathfrak{G}$.

Our group $\mathfrak{G}_8$ can, therefore, only contain non-trivial subgroups with 2 or 4 elements. The following is a complete enumeration of the subgroups of $\mathfrak{G}_8$.

$$\{I, R_2\}, \{I, M_1\}, \{I, M_2\}, \{I, M_3\}, \{I, M_4\},$$
$$\{I, R_1, R_2, R_3\}, \{I, R_2, M_1, M_2\}, \{I, R_2, M_3, M_4\}.$$

The subgroup $\{I, M_1\}$ is characterized geometrically by the fact that the vertices B and D are fixed points under mappings of this group.* Try to characterize the remaining subgroups of $\mathfrak{G}_8$ in this way.

According to the particular field of mathematics which has given rise to the group in question, this theorem contains a number theoretic, algebraic or geometric statement—the group concept reveals common mathematical structures.

We now wish to connect our group $\mathfrak{G}_8$ with a group of permutations. Here we touch upon the field of mathematics where the idea of a group first appeared.

If we only consider the four vertices A, B, C, D of our square, every isometry in $\mathfrak{G}_8$ produces a one-one mapping of the point set $\{A, B, C, D\}$ onto itself. We have already mentioned on p. 19 that such one-one mappings of a finite point set onto itself are called permutations.†

Our group of isometries which leave the square invariant consist of permutations which preserve relations of proximity. That is, in the square the vertices A and C are adjoining B; this property is preserved by mappings of $\mathfrak{G}_8$. There are other

* This is another example of the previously mentioned fact that the choice of a subgroup corresponds to an increase in the invariants. Now not only is the square as a whole invariant but also two vertices stay fixed.

† Often the actual result of the mapping, that is, a particular order of the elements, is called a permutation.

permutations of $\{A, B, C, D\}$ apart from the eight in $\mathfrak{G}_8$. For example, the permutation

$$\Psi = \begin{Bmatrix} A & B & C & D \\ B & D & A & C \end{Bmatrix}$$

does not occur in $\mathfrak{G}_8$; after this mapping C and D are the adjoining points to B (we must think of the cyclic order of the four points). Altogether there are as many permutations of four elements as the number of different orders of these elements. This number is

$$4.3.2.1 = 4! = 24,$$

for we have four possible choices for the first place, for the second place there are three choices, for the third place we have two elements to choose from, and the remaining element goes into the fourth place. The 24 permutations of the four elements A, B, C, D can be characterized by the second line of our permutation symbol; in alphabetical order they are:

ABCD (*r*)	*BACD*	*CABD*	*DABC* (*r*)
ABDC	*BADC* (*m*)	*CADB*	*DACB*
ACBD	*BCAD*	*CBAD* (*m*)	*DBAC*
ACDB	*BCDA* (*r*)	*CBDA*	*DBCA*
ADBC	*BDAC*	*CDAB* (*r*)	*DCAB*
ADCB (*m*)	*BDCA*	*CDBA*	*DCBA* (*m*)

These permutations form a group of which our group of mappings, $\mathfrak{G}_8$, is a subgroup. We verify again in this example that the number of elements in a subgroup is a divisor of the number of elements in the full group; 8 is a divisor of 24. In the table of the 24 permutations, the rotations are denoted by (*r*) and the reflections by (*m*).

Problem 65. Find the group table of the isometries which map an equilateral triangle onto itself.

Problem 66. The two permutations

$$\Psi_1 = \begin{Bmatrix} A & B & C & D & E & F & G & H \\ C & H & D & F & B & A & G & E \end{Bmatrix}$$

$$\text{and } \Psi_2 = \begin{Bmatrix} A & B & C & D & E & F & G & H \\ C & D & A & B & E & F & G & H \end{Bmatrix}$$

are elements of the group of permutations of eight objects.

(a) Determine the permutations Ψ_1^{-1}, Ψ_2^{-1}, Ψ_2^{2}.

(b) Determine the permutations $\Psi_1\Psi_2$, $\Psi_2\Psi_1$ and $\Psi_1\Psi_2\Psi_1^{-1}$.

(c) Show that Ψ_2 is an involution;

(d) Which is the smallest exponent p for which $\Psi_1^{p} = I$?

(e) Show that the elements $\Psi_1, \Psi_1^{2}, \Psi_1^{3}, \ldots, \Psi_1^{p-1}, \Psi_1^{p} = I$ form a group.

For the solution of (d) consider a set of eight points and indicate the mapping defined by Ψ_1 (see Figure 55). From the cycles appearing in this figure we can easily compute p.

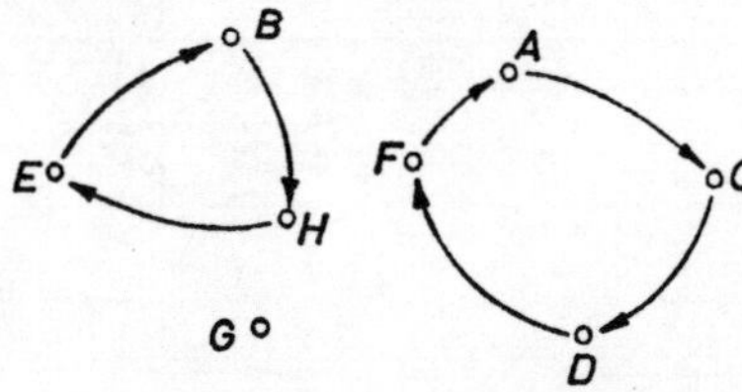

Fig. 55

Problem 67. Consider each capital letter of the alphabet in turn and find the group of isometries which map the figure onto itself. Divide the letters into classes by putting all letters having the same group of isometries into the same class.

Fig 56

Problem 68. Repeat Problem 67 for the frieze patterns shown in Figure 56 which we imagine to be extended indefinitely in both directions.

Problem 69. Verify the relation

$$(\Phi\Psi)^{-1} = \Psi^{-1}\Phi^{-1},$$

which holds for all groups, and give some examples taken from the groups we have considered.

7

ENLARGEMENTS

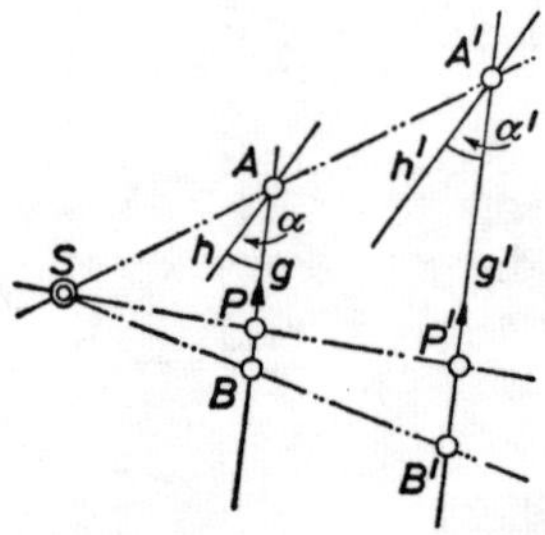

Fig. 57

Let S be a fixed point in the plane and μ a non-zero number (positive or negative). We define a mapping of the plane by the following rules:

A point A and its image A' lie on the same straight line through S, that is, A, A' and S are collinear.

Moreover, each pair A, A' satisfy the relation

$$\frac{SA'}{SA} = \mu \qquad \textit{(here we think of directed line segments).}$$

This mapping is called an *enlargement*. S is the *centre* and μ the *scale factor* of the enlargement. If $\mu > 0$, the corresponding points A and A' lie on the same side of S. If, however, $\mu < 0$, then S lies between A and A'. An enlargement with scale factor -1 is the same as a half-turn about S.

If we are given S, A and A', then it is easy to construct the image of any other point B (see Figure 57). We draw the line through A' parallel to AB to intersect SB in B'.

We then have,

$$\frac{SB'}{SB} = \frac{SA'}{SA} = \mu.$$

It is just as easy to find the original point B if we are given the image point B'. The construction shows that enlargement is a one-one mapping. In general, S is the only fixed point of the transformation.

Here is a list of other properties of enlargements which will be used in later constructions.

From Figure 57 we can see that if a point P moves on the line g, only the ray of projection SP' will change in the drawing. In particular, the parallel g' remains fixed. This means that if P moves along g, its image P' will describe the line g'; g' is, therefore, the image of g.

1. Enlargements are line-preserving transformations. Moreover, a line g and its image g' are always parallel.

We note that lines through S are mapped onto themselves, although not all their points stay in the same place. They are fixed lines but not pointwise fixed.

As each pair g, g' and h, h' of corresponding lines is parallel, the angle between g and h is preserved by the transformation; in other words:

2. Enlargements are angle-preserving transformations.

We have, further, the relation

$$\frac{SA'}{SA} = \frac{A'B'}{AB} = \mu,$$

which means:

3. The lengths of corresponding line segments are in the ratio $1:\mu$.

If $\mu > 0$, corresponding line segments are parallel in the same sense; if $\mu < 0$ they are parallel but are in the opposite sense.

We deduce immediately the following property:

4. The ratio of the lengths of two image line segments is equal to the ratio of the lengths of the original line segments. Thus, enlargements preserve ratios of distances.

In a triangle and its image under enlargement the altitudes are also corresponding line segments, hence the areas are in the ratio $1:\mu^2$. Since polygons can be divided into triangles, and figures with a curved boundary can be approximated arbitrarily closely by means of polygons, we have:

5. The areas of a figure and its image under an enlargement are in the ratio $1:\mu^2$.

Further, we have:

6. The inverse transformation to an enlargement $E(S,\mu)$ is the enlargement $E^{-1}(S, 1/\mu)$.

We shall now look at a series of problems which can be solved by enlargements applied to a geometric locus.

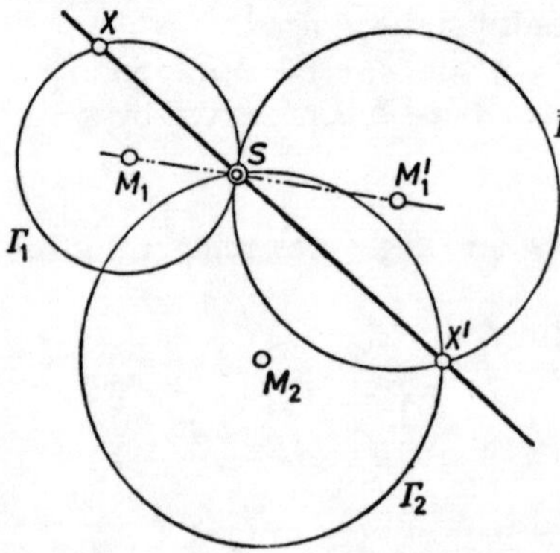

Fig. 58

Problem 70. Construct a line through one point of intersection, S, of two circles Γ_1 and Γ_2, such that the two chords on this line have lengths in the ratio 2:3.

Let X and X' be the other points of intersection of the required line with the circles Γ_1 and Γ_2 (see Figure 58). Then we can write

$$\frac{SX'}{SX} = -\frac{3}{2}.$$

Hence, X' is the point of intersection of Γ_2 with the image of Γ_1 under the enlargement with centre S and scale factor $-3/2$.

The enlargement with scale factor 3/2 gives another solution; in this case one of the chords lies on the other.

Problem 71. Given are two squares with a common vertex A. Draw a line through A such that the lengths of the segments inside the squares are in the ratio 1:2.

Problem 72. Given are two circles Γ_1 and Γ_2, and a point S. Construct a point A on Γ_1 and a point B on Γ_2 such that S is the mid-point of AB.

Problem 73. Construct the triangle ABC, given the lengths of the sides AB and AC, and the length of the bisector of $\angle BAC$.

Let $AB = c$, $AC = b$ and let the length of the angle bisector AW be w. We begin the construction by drawing AW. A geometric locus for B is the circle Γ with centre A and radius c (see Figure 59). Now we know that W divides BC in the ratio $c{:}b$. An enlargement with centre W and scale factor $-b/c$ will, therefore, map Γ onto a geometric locus for the vertex C. On the other hand, C must lie on the circle with centre A and radius b.

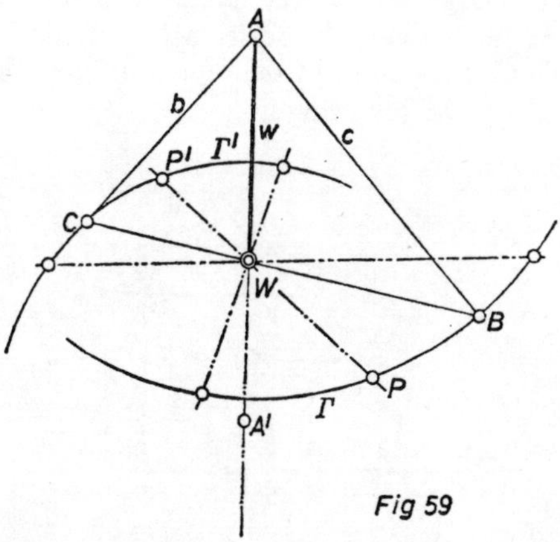

Fig 59

Problem 74. Construct a triangle ABC in which BC is of length a, the median from B is of length m, and the lengths of the sides AC and BA are in the ratio $1:\lambda$.

We start by drawing the line segment BC. The Apollonius circle Γ defined by $BP:PC = \lambda:1$ is then a geometric locus for A. An enlargement with centre C and scale factor $\frac{1}{2}$ maps Γ into a geometric locus for the mid-point A' of AC. However, A' also lies on the circle with centre B and radius m.

Problem 75. Construct a triangle ABC given the lengths of the sides AC and AB, and the length s of the median from A.

We begin the construction by drawing $AB = c$. The circle Γ with centre A and radius b ($= AC$) is then a geometric locus for C. This can be transformed into a locus for C', the mid-point of BC, by an enlargement with centre B and scale factor $\frac{1}{2}$. Another locus for C' is given by s.

If we begin the construction by drawing the line segment AC', then the problem can be solved by using a half-turn.

In the following examples enlargements are used in an essentially different way. The common method of solution is by relaxing one, or possibly more, of the conditions. This is done in such a way that the remaining conditions determine a family of figures which can be mapped onto each other by enlargements. After constructing one member of this family, we transform it by an enlargement so that its image satisfies the omitted conditions as well. Thus, the scale factor of the enlargement used depends on the choice of the representative, that is, upon the way we draw the initial figure.

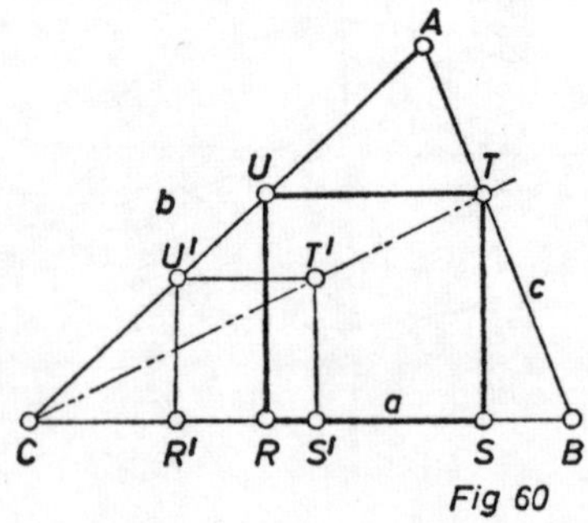

Fig 60

Problem 76. Given a triangle ABC, construct a square with two vertices on BC and one vertex on each of the sides AB and AC.

If we ignore the condition that T should lie on AB, a family of squares is determined. The square $R'S'T'U'$ (see Figure 60) is one representative of this family. By a suitable enlargement with centre C, we can map T' onto T without disturbing the other incidences. The scale factor of this enlargement depends upon the choice of $R'S'T'U'$.

We leave it to the reader to show that the problem could also be solved using enlargements with centre A and with centre B.

Problem 77. Draw a circle to pass through two given points A and B and to intersect the given line s in a chord which subtends an angle of 120° at the centre of the circle.

The centre M of the circle to be constructed lies on m, the mediator of AB (see Figure 61). We first consider the family of all circles with centres on m which satisfy the condition on their intersection with s. This is a family of circles which can be mapped onto one another by enlargements with centre S, the point of intersection of m and s. By a suitable mapping of a representative circle Γ' we can obtain a circle Γ which satisfies all the given conditions. Note that the problem has two solutions, since there are two points A_1' and A'_2 on Γ' which can be mapped onto A. Figure 61 shows only one solution.

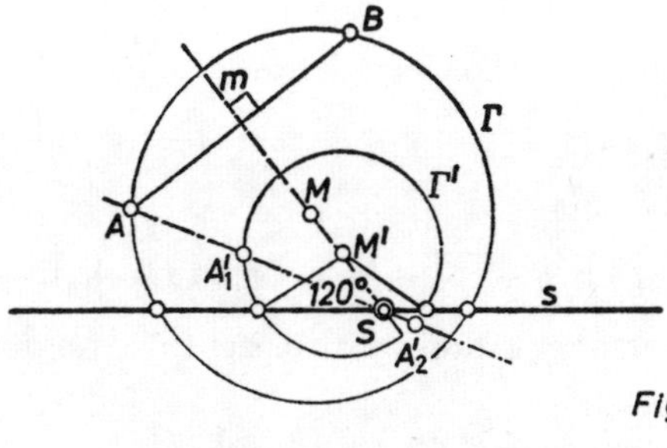

Fig 61

THE GROUP PROPERTIES OF ENLARGEMENTS

We now investigate the transformation obtained by combining two enlargements. Assume that:

E_1 is an enlargement with centre S_1 and scale factor μ_1;
E_2 is an enlargement with centre S_2 and scale factor μ_2.

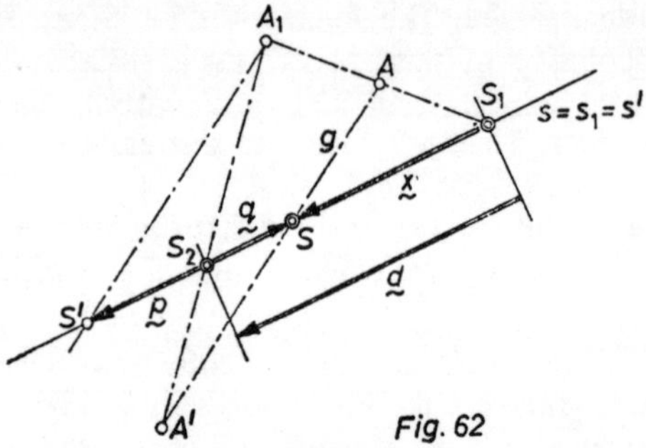

Fig. 62

A point A is mapped onto A_1 by E_1, and A_1 is mapped onto A' by E_2 (see Figure 62). The transformation E_2E_1 leaves the line s through S_1 and S_2 fixed, since s is a fixed line for both enlargements. The image of an arbitrary line h through A is parallel to h and through A'. From this it follows immediately that the line g, joining A to A', is another fixed line of E_2E_1. The point S where the lines g and s meet is, therefore, a fixed point of E_2E_1. We now want to calculate the position of S on s. In order to do this we introduce the following vectors:

$$S_1S_2 = \mathbf{d}, \quad S_2S' = \mathbf{p} \text{ (S' is the image of S under E_1)},$$
$$S_1S = \mathbf{x}, \quad S_2S = \mathbf{q}.$$

Then we have the following relations:

$$\mathbf{p}+\mathbf{d} = \mu_1\mathbf{x}, \quad \mathbf{q} = \mu_2\mathbf{p}, \quad \mathbf{d}+\mathbf{q} = \mathbf{x}.$$

From these we obtain

$$\mathbf{x} = \mathbf{d}+\mathbf{q} = \mathbf{d}+\mu_2\mathbf{p} = \mathbf{d}+\mu_2(\mu_1\mathbf{x}-\mathbf{d}) = (1-\mu_2)\mathbf{d}+\mu_1\mu_2\mathbf{x}.$$

Solving this vector equation with respect to $\mathbf{x}$, we obtain

$$\mathbf{x} = \frac{1-\mu_2}{1-\mu_1\mu_2}\mathbf{d}.*$$

* The position of S relative to S_1 and S_2 can also be represented by the fraction $\lambda = \frac{SS_1}{SS_2}$. We find $\lambda = \frac{1-\mu_2}{\mu_1\mu_2-\mu_2}$.

This shows that S does not depend upon the choice of A; S is determined by the two mappings E_1 and E_2. For the transformation E_2E_1, therefore, corresponding pairs of points A, A' lie on lines through the fixed point S.

From Figure 62 we can also recognize the following relation:

$$\frac{SA'}{SA} = \frac{S'A_1}{SA} \cdot \frac{SA'}{S'A_1} = \mu_1\mu_2.$$

Hence, we have shown that E_2E_1 is an enlargement with centre S and scale factor $\mu = \mu_1\mu_2$.

The product of two enlargements E_1 and E_2 is, in general, again an enlargement, E. The three centres S_1, S_2 and S are collinear, and the scale factors satisfy the relation $\mu = \mu_1\mu_2$.

In Figure 63 this result is illustrated by the transformation of the triangle ABC. A new group of mappings begins to be recognizable.

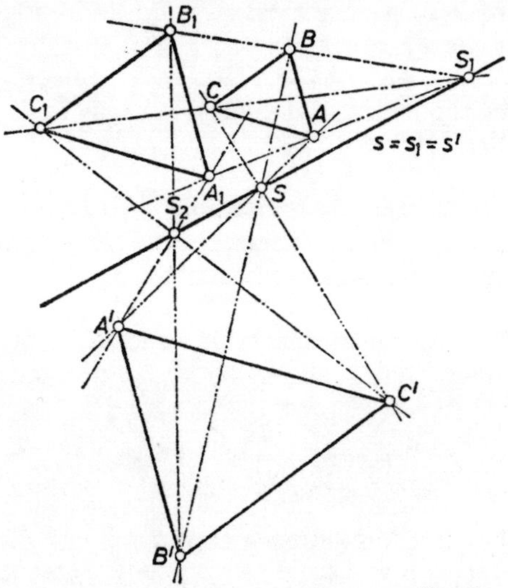

Fig 63

Problem 78. Given are two enlargements $E_1(S_1,2)$ and $E_2(S_2, -2/3)$. Construct and calculate the position of S, the centre of the mapping E_2E_1.

To construct S, map an arbitrary point A (which does not lie on the line S_1S_2) by E_2E_1. The position of S can be calculated by the vector formula given above. Here we have

$$\boldsymbol{x} = \frac{1-(-2/3)}{1-2(-2/3)}\boldsymbol{d} = \frac{5}{7}\boldsymbol{d}.$$

Problem 79. Find the product of the two enlargements $E_1(S_1,2)$ and $E_2(S_2,\frac{1}{2})$.

If we apply the transformation E_2E_1 to a point A we obtain a situation like that shown in Figure 64. It can be seen that for every pair of corresponding points A and A', the vector from A to A' is $\boldsymbol{v} = \frac{1}{2}\boldsymbol{d}$. Hence, E_2E_1 is obviously a translation with the vector $\boldsymbol{v}$.

Since, for our pair of enlargements, $\mu_1\mu_2 = 1$, the denominator in our formula for $\boldsymbol{x}$ vanishes. If the value of $\mu_1\mu_2$ is very close to 1, then the vector $\boldsymbol{x}$ will be very long. We can take $\mu_1\mu_2 = 1$ to characterize the point at infinity on the line through S_1 and S_2.*

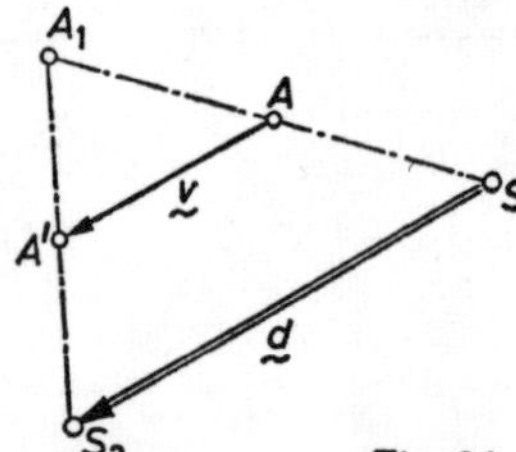

Fig. 64

We can now .consider translations to be special cases of enlargements; the centre of enlargement for a translation is a point at infinity and the scale factor is 1.

Problem 80. Two enlargements E_1 and E_2 are given with $\mu_1\mu_2 = 1$. Show that $\boldsymbol{v}$, the vector of the translation E_2E_1, is given by

$$\boldsymbol{v} = \left(1-\frac{1}{\mu_1}\right)\boldsymbol{d} = (1-\mu_2)\boldsymbol{d}.$$

Problem 81. T is a translation with vector $\boldsymbol{v}$ and E an enlargement with centre S and scale factor $\mu \neq 1$. Show that ET and TE are enlargements with scale factor μ and construct the centres of these transformations.

* The point at infinity is not a proper point. We consider it as an ideal element corresponding to the value $\lambda = 1$ for the ratio of distances of a point from two given points.

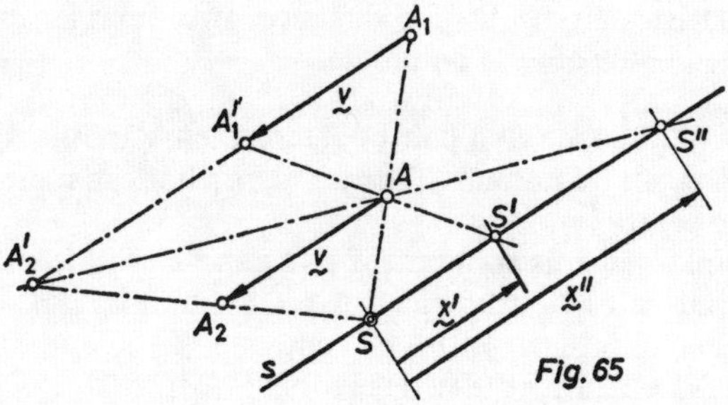

Fig. 65

We can use the same method as in the case of the two finite enlargements. The line through S parallel to $\boldsymbol{v}$ is a fixed line of $TE = E'$ and $ET = E''$. In Figure 65 the centres S' of E' and S'' of E'' have been obtained by finding the images of a point A. It is easy to verify that

$$\boldsymbol{x}' = -\frac{1}{\mu - 1}\boldsymbol{v} \quad \text{and} \quad \boldsymbol{x}'' = -\frac{\mu}{\mu - 1}\boldsymbol{v}.$$

If we use the equivalence

$$E' = TE \Leftrightarrow E'E^{-1} = T,$$

and the corresponding one for E'', then these relations can be deduced from the result of Problem 80.

Theorem 14. The set of all enlargements forms a group, $\mathfrak{A}$, under the operation of combination of transformations.

To prove this we must show that the group postulates are all satisfied. When we consider the product of two elements of $\mathfrak{A}$ we have to consider the possibility of the transformations being translations.

The unit element of $\mathfrak{A}$ is the identity I. As in the case of rotations, I can be represented in different ways; every enlargement with $\mu = 1$ represents I provided the centre of enlargement is a finite point.

The group is not commutative; this means that, in general, a product depends on the order of the factors. We give as an example of two elements which do not commute, the two transformations T and E of Problem 81. There are, of course, commutative pairs in $\mathfrak{A}$; for instance, two enlargements with the same centre always commute.

Problem 82. Show that a pair of enlargements, neither of which is a translation, commute if, and only if, both mappings have the same centre.

Two enlargements commute if E_2E_1 and E_1E_2 have the same centre. This is obviously true if $S_1 = S_2$, that is, if $\boldsymbol{d} = 0$.

Now assume that $\boldsymbol{d} \neq 0$. The centres of E_2E_1 and E_1E_2 can then be described by the two vectors

$$\boldsymbol{x}' = \frac{1-\mu_2}{1-\mu_1\mu_2}\boldsymbol{d} \quad \text{and} \quad \boldsymbol{x}'' = -\frac{1-\mu_1}{1-\mu_1\mu_2}\boldsymbol{d}.$$

$\boldsymbol{x}'$ and $\boldsymbol{x}''$ describe the same point if $\boldsymbol{x}'-\boldsymbol{x}'' = \boldsymbol{d}$ (see Figure 66), that is, if

$$\frac{1-\mu_1}{1-\mu_1\mu_2}+\frac{1-\mu_2}{1-\mu_1\mu_2} = 1.$$

This equation can be transformed to

$$(1-\mu_1)(1-\mu_2) = 0.$$

But this can never hold since $\mu_1 \neq 1$ and $\mu_2 \neq 1$.

If $\mu_1\mu_2 = 1$, it can easily be deduced from the formula in Problem 80 that the two translations E_2E_1 and E_1E_2 have different vectors (unless $\mu_1+\mu_2 = 2$, in which case $\mu_1 = \mu_2 = 1$).

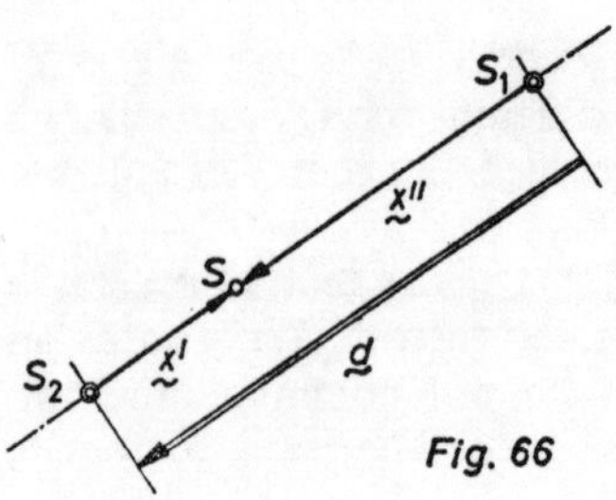

Fig. 66

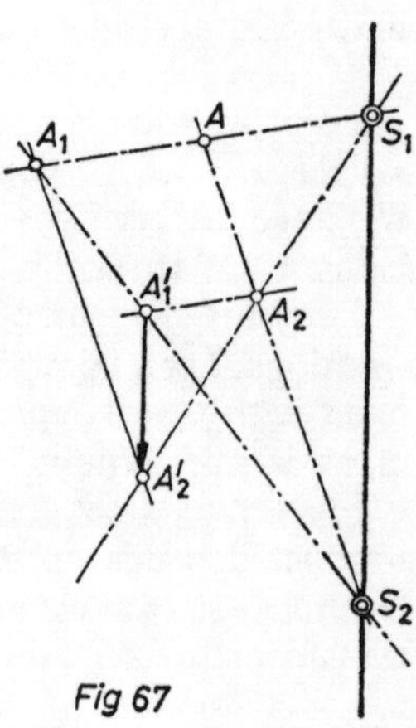

Fig 67

Problem 83. An enlargement E_1 with centre S_1 maps A onto A_1. A second enlargement E_2 with centre S_2 maps A_1 onto A_1'. Hence, A_1' is the image of A under the transformation E_2E_1. Construct the image of A under the transformation E_1E_2.

We give the solution without comment in Figure 67.

Problem 84. If E_1 and E_2 are two enlargements, show that

$$E_1E_2(E_2E_1)^{-1} = E_1E_2E_1^{-1}E_2^{-1}$$

is always a translation T with a vector $\boldsymbol{v}$ which has the direction of the line joining S_1 and S_2.

This is illustrated in Figure 67; T maps the point A_1' onto A_2'.

Try to express the translation vector of T in terms of μ_1, μ_2 and $\boldsymbol{d} = S_1S_2$.

Problem 85. Two enlargements $E_1(S_1, \mu_1)$ and $E_2(S_2, \mu_2)$ are given. Construct the centre of the mapping $E_1E_2E_1^{-1}$.

Problem 86. Construct the centre of the transformation $E_3E_2E_1$, where E_1, E_2 and E_3 are three given enlargements, and illustrate geometrically by means of this figure that the associative law holds in $\mathfrak{A}$, that is

$$E_3(E_2E_1) = (E_3E_2)E_1.$$

What incidences can be derived from this?

Problem 87. Prove the following theorem of Menelaus: If a line s intersects the sides of a triangle A, A', A^* in the points S_1, S_2, S_3, then

$$\frac{S_1A'}{S_1A}\cdot\frac{S_2A^*}{S_2A'}\cdot\frac{S_3A}{S_3A^*} = 1.$$

To prove this we introduce the following three enlargements:

$$E_1\left(S_1, \mu_1 = \frac{S_1A'}{S_1A}\right); E_2\left(S_2, \mu_2 = \frac{S_2A^*}{S_2A'}\right); E_3\left(S_3, \mu_3 = \frac{S_3A}{S_3A^*}\right).$$

The enlargements with centres on a line s form a subgroup of $\mathfrak{A}$; this is a simple consequence of the rules for composition.

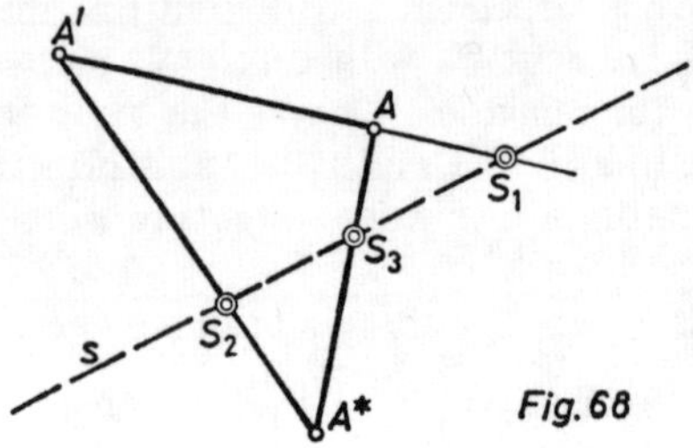

Fig. 68

We shall denote this subgroup by $\mathfrak{A}_s$.

Then $E_3E_2E_1 \in \mathfrak{A}_s$. But A, which does not lie on s, is a fixed point of this mapping. This can only happen if the mapping is the identity. However,

$$E_3E_2E_1 = I \Rightarrow \mu_1\mu_2\mu_3 = 1,$$

which proves our theorem.

Problem 88. Prove the following theorem of Desargues: If the lines joining corresponding vertices of the triangles ABC and $A'B'C'$ are parallel, then the points of intersection of corresponding sides lie on a line s.

The proof, like that of Problem 87, can be reduced to the composition of transformations in $\mathfrak{A}$.

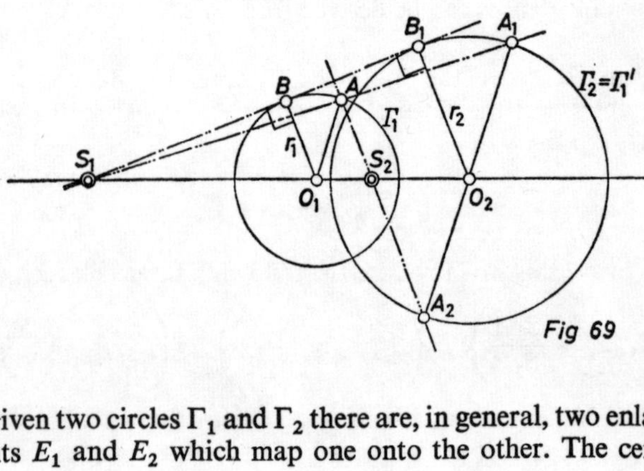

Fig 69

Given two circles Γ_1 and Γ_2 there are, in general, two enlargements E_1 and E_2 which map one onto the other. The centres

S_1 and S_2 lie on the line through the centres of the circles;* the easiest way of finding them is by using parallel radii of the circles (see Figure 69). The corresponding scale factors are

$$\mu_1 = \frac{r_2}{r_1} \quad \text{and} \quad \mu_2 = -\frac{r_2}{r_1}.$$

Problem 89. Show that the six centres of enlargement associated with the three circles $\Gamma_1, \Gamma_2, \Gamma_3$, lie on four lines, three on each line. (Theorem of Monge.)

We pick out two circles Γ_i and Γ_j. There are two enlargements E_{ij} and E_{ij}' which map Γ_i onto Γ_j; let E_{ij} be the one with a positive scale factor. We immediately deduce the following relations:

$$E_{23}E_{12} = E_{13}, \qquad E_{23}E_{12}' = E_{13}',$$
$$E_{23}'E_{12} = E_{13}', \qquad E_{23}'E_{12}' = E_{13},$$

which imply the statement to be proved.

Problem 90. There are two enlargements E and E^* which map the circle Γ onto the given circle Γ'. Describe the mapping E^*E^{-1}.

The following four problems provide a method, based on transformation geometry, for proving Feuerbach's Theorem on the so-called nine-point circle.

Problem 91. Show that, in every triangle, the point of intersection of the altitudes H (the orthocentre), the centroid G, and the circumcentre O lie on a line (the Euler line).

Hint: use the enlargement which maps the given triangle ABC onto the triangle $A'B'C'$ formed by the mid-points of the sides of ABC.

Problem 92. Show that the circumcentre O' of the triangle $A'B'C'$ lies on the Euler line of the triangle ABC.

Problem 93. Denote the circumcircles of ABC and $A'B'C'$ by Γ and Γ' respectively. They can be mapped onto each other by two enlargements:

* S_1 and S_2 are often referred to as centres of similitude.

$$E(G, -\tfrac{1}{2}) \text{ and } E^*(G^*, \tfrac{1}{2}).$$

Show that the centre of enlargement G^* is H.

Problem 94. The image of the triangle ABC under E^* is a triangle $A^*B^*C^*$. A^*, B^* and C^* are the mid-points of the lines joining H to the vertices A, B and C.

Note that (A', A^*), (B', B^*) and (C', C^*) are pairs of corresponding points under the transformation E^*E^{-1} and use this to prove that the circle Γ' passes through the feet of the altitudes of the triangle ABC.

The circle Γ' has now been shown to contain the mid-points of the sides, the feet of the altitudes, and the mid-points of the lines joining the orthocentre to the three vertices—Γ' is Feuerbach's nine-point circle.

SUBGROUPS OF $\mathfrak{A}$

We have already mentioned that:

The enlargements with centres on a fixed line g form a subgroup $\mathfrak{A}_g$ of $\mathfrak{A}$. The transformations of $\mathfrak{A}_g$ are distinguished by the fact that they all leave the line g invariant.

If two enlargements have the same centre G, that is, if $\boldsymbol{d} = 0$, then $\boldsymbol{x} = 0$. Hence, the centre of the product is G also. We conclude that the transformations of $\mathfrak{A}$ with a given centre G also form a subgroup $\mathfrak{A}_G$. Its elements are characterized by the invariance of the point G. If G lies on g, then

$$\mathfrak{A}_G \subset \mathfrak{A}_g,$$

that is, $\mathfrak{A}_G$ is a subgroup of $\mathfrak{A}_g$.

We noted earlier that subgroups can be obtained by demanding additional invariants. $\mathfrak{A}_g$ is obtained from $\mathfrak{A}$ by demanding that the arbitrary line g is invariant, and $\mathfrak{A}_G$ by demanding that the point G is invariant.

We can also demand the invariance of a whole figure. We may, for example, imagine the square and circle pattern shown in Figure 70 to be continued indefinitely in both directions. This leads to a figure which is invariant under enlargements with centre S and scale factor $(\sqrt{2})^n$ where n is any integer. These mappings form a subgroup $\mathfrak{A}_S'$ of $\mathfrak{A}_S$ and therefore of $\mathfrak{A}$ itself. Unlike the previous examples $\mathfrak{A}_S'$ is a discrete subgroup of $\mathfrak{A}$.

By this we mean that the transformations in $\mathfrak{A}_S'$ do not form a continuous family.

The most general enlargements leaving Figure 70 invariant have scale factors $\pm(\sqrt{2})^n$ where n is any integer. These mappings form a group $\mathfrak{A}_S''$ and we have the chain of inclusions:

$$\mathfrak{A}_S' \subset \mathfrak{A}_S'' \subset \mathfrak{A}_S \subset \mathfrak{A}.$$

All these subgroups of $\mathfrak{A}$ have infinitely many elements.

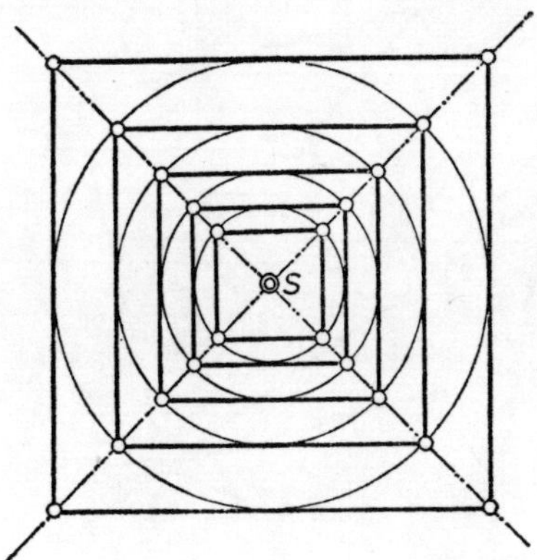

Fig. 70

8

SIMILARITIES

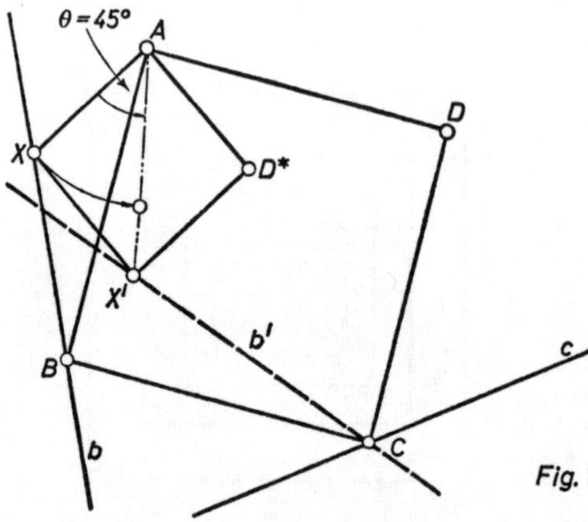

Fig. 71

Problem 95. A point A and lines b and c are given. Construct a square with A as a vertex such that the vertex B lies on b and the vertex C on c. C is the vertex opposite A.*

To solve this we first disregard the condition that C should lie on c. We then get a family of squares of which $AXX'D^*$ is a representative (see Figure 71). In this we can think of X' as the image of X under a rotation about A through 45°, followed by an enlargement with centre A and scale factor $\sqrt{2}$. If X′ moves on the line b', the image of b under these two transformations, then C is the intersection of b' and c. The rotation with $\theta = -45°$ leads to a second solution of the problem.

This method of solution is based on transforming a geometric locus; we have used this method before. What is new is that here two different types of transformations have been

* Cf. Problem 23 in which similar conditions were given.

combined—the transformation used was the product of a rotation and an enlargement having the same centre. It is easy to see that the two mappings commute; it does not matter whether the rotation or the enlargement is performed first.

We call the product of a rotation and an enlargement with the same centre S a *spiral similarity*.

This defines a new type of transformation. A spiral similarity is characterized by the centre S, the angle of rotation θ, and the scale factor μ; we may denote it by $W(S,\theta,\mu)$. Before we turn to the theory of spiral similarities we give two further construction problems of the same type as Problem 95.

Problem 96. Given are a point A and two lines b and c. Construct a triangle ABC with B on b, C on c, $\angle BAC = 60°$ and $\angle ABC = 45°$.

A procedure analogous to that used in Problem 95 leads to a spiral similarity $W(A, \pm 60°, \sin 45°/\sin 75°)$.

Problem 97. Given are a point A, a circle Γ and a line g. Construct a rectangle with sides in the ratio 1:2, which has one vertex at A, the vertex B on Γ and the vertex C (opposite to A) on g. AB is to be one of the shorter sides of the rectangle.

The solution to this problem uses a spiral similarity

$$W(A, \pm \tan^{-1}2, \sqrt{5}).$$

The angle of rotation and the scale factor can be constructed in a model figure.

Problem 98. Given are four points A, B, C, D. Find a rectangle with sides in the ratio 1:2, such that each side (or its extension) passes through one of the given points.

This is a generalization of Problem 45. Now the strip bounded by a and c is mapped onto the strip bounded by b and d (see Figure 72) by the spiral similarity

$$W(M, 90°, 2).$$

The vector $\boldsymbol{u}$ is mapped onto a vector $\boldsymbol{w}$ which is orthogonal to $\boldsymbol{u}$ and twice as long. The translation T with vector $\boldsymbol{t}$ maps the image C' $(= W(C))$ onto D. If we draw $\boldsymbol{w}$ with end-point D,

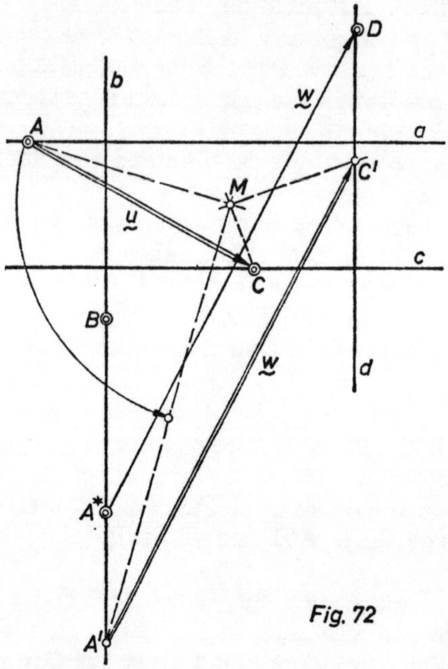

Fig. 72

then the starting point A^* is a point of the side b of our rectangle. A^* and B together determine b and it is then easy to complete the rectangle.

In solving Problem 98 we had to use the product of a spiral similarity and a translation. This means we multiplied an enlargement by a rotation and a translation.

Definition. A finite product of isometries and enlargements is called a *similarity*.

Similarities, like isometries, can be divided into two classes, *direct* (orientation preserving) similarities and *opposite* (orientation reversing) similarities.

DIRECT SIMILARITIES

The spiral similarity is an example of a direct similarity. If

$R(S,\theta)$ is a rotation and $E(S,\mu)$ is an enlargement, then

$$ER = RE = W(S,\theta,\mu)$$

is a spiral similarity with centre S, angle of rotation θ, and scale factor μ.

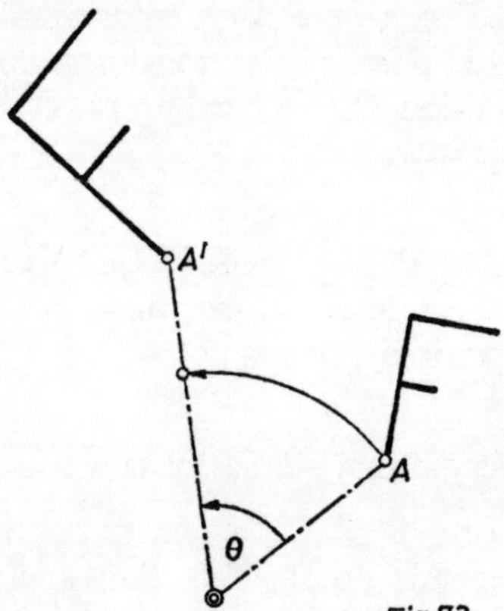

Fig 73

For spiral similarities we have the relation

$$W(S,\theta,\mu) = W(S,\theta+\pi,-\mu).$$

In order to obtain a unique representation, we shall always assume that $\mu>0$ in what follows.

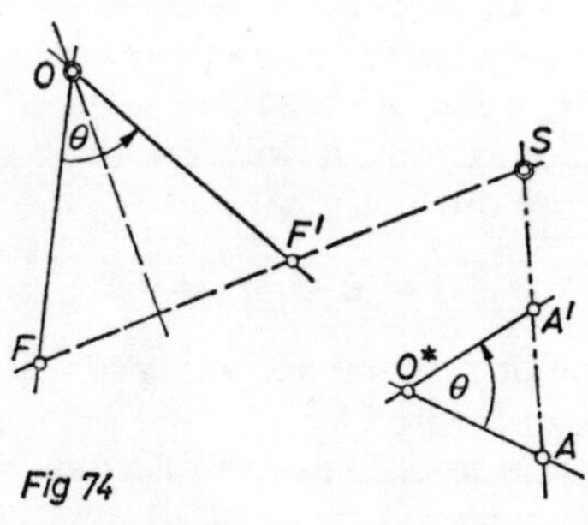

Fig 74

Problem 99. Let K be a direct isometry and E an enlargement with centre S and scale factor $\mu \neq 1$. Show that the direct similarity $\Omega = EK$ always has a fixed point F.

We first assume that K is a rotation with centre O through angle θ (see Figure 74). We can always find a point F which is mapped onto the same image F' by both K and E^{-1}. To do this we take two corresponding points A and A' ($= E^{-1}(A)$) and draw the isosceles triangle with angle $AO^*A' = \theta$. The triangle AO^*A' is mapped onto FOF' by a spiral similarity with centre S. F is now a fixed point of the transformation EK.

If K is a translation, then a fixed point can be constructed in an equally simple way.

The definition of similarities may lead us to expect to find many different types of transformations in the class of direct similarities. Surprisingly, this is not so; we can show:

Theorem 15. Every direct similarity is a spiral similarity.

The proof depends on the fact that a direct similarity is completely determined by two points A and B, and their images A' and B'.

If the line segment $A'B'$ is congruent to AB, then Ω, the transformation mapping AB onto $A'B'$, is a translation or a rotation. Both are special cases of spiral similarities.

We now assume that AB and $A'B'$ are not congruent. Let p be the mediator of AA'. The reflection M_p maps A onto A'; we denote the image of B under this mapping by B^*. We now introduce q, the bisector of the angle between $A'B^*$ and $A'B'$. The reflection M_q leaves A' fixed and maps B^* onto $B\dagger$. If we denote by E the enlargement with centre A' and scale factor $\mu = B'A'/B\dagger A'$, we obviously have

$$\Omega = EM_qM_p = EK.$$

K is a translation or rotation according to whether p and q are parallel or not (see Figure 75).

We now have the situation of Problem 99. We know, therefore, that the mapping Ω has a fixed point F. The isometry $K = M_qM_p$ can also be obtained as the product of two different reflections; if we choose p_1 to be the line through O and F we have to use as q_1 the perpendicular through O to the line s

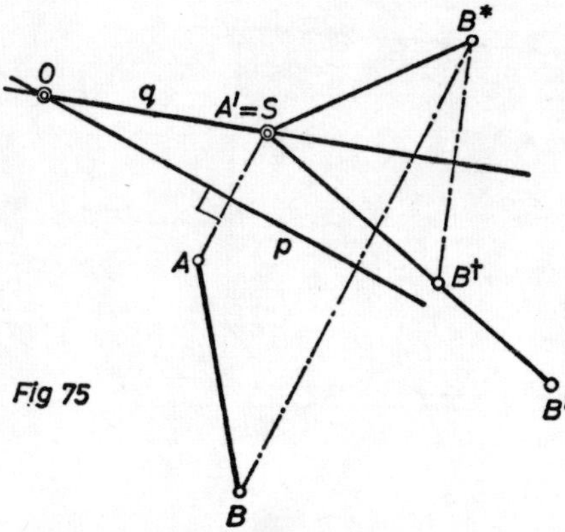

Fig 75

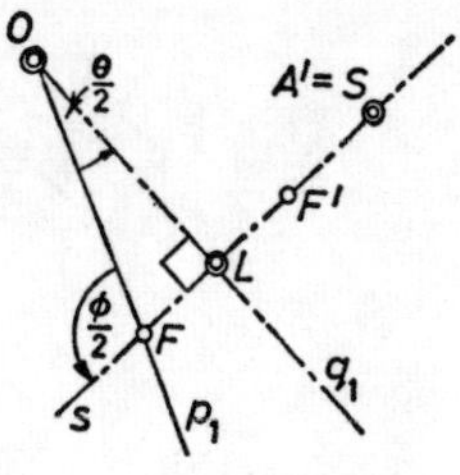

Fig 76

joining A' and F.† In order not to overcomplicate Figure 75, these extensions are shown in Figure 76. We now have

$$\Omega = EM_qM_p = EM_{q_1}M_{p_1} = E(M_{q_1}M_s)(M_sM_{p_1}).$$

The introduction of $M_s^2 = I$ does not, of course, change the transformation. $M_sM_{p_1}$ is a rotation with centre F and $M_{q_1}M_s$ represents a half-turn, H_L, which we can also interpret as an enlargement. From the rule for combining enlargements, we know that EH_L is an enlargement with its centre on s. But F and F' are corresponding points for both E and H_L; hence EH_L leaves the point F fixed. Therefore, F is the centre of enlargement of $EH_L = E^*$.

Thus we have obtained a representation

$$\Omega = E^*(F,-\mu)R(F,\phi) = W(F,\phi,-\mu) = W(F,\theta,\mu).$$

Ω is a spiral similarity with centre F.

Problem 100. A, A' and B, B' are corresponding pairs of points for the spiral similarity

$$W(S,\theta,\mu).$$

Determine the centre S, the angle of rotation θ, and the scale factor μ.

† In the case of a translation, p_1 is the perpendicular to s through F.

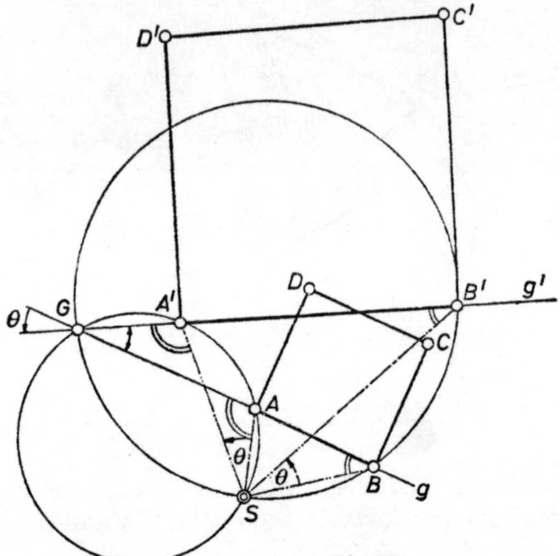

Fig. 77

θ appears as the angle between corresponding lines g and g', and $\mu = A'B'/AB$.

If A and A' are corresponding points, then $\angle ASA' = \theta$. Using this property we can find S by the construction indicated in Figure 77.

The product of two direct similarities is again a direct similarity. If we consider translations and enlargements as special cases of spiral similarities, then we can state our result as follows:

Theorem 16. The spiral similarities form a group $\mathfrak{S}$ under the operation of combination of transformations.

The group $\mathfrak{S}$ contains as subgroups, the group $\mathfrak{A}$ of enlargements, the group $\mathfrak{K}$ of isometries and the group $\mathfrak{T}$ of translations.

Problem 101. Discuss the construction considered in Problem 100 for special positions of the points A, A' and B, B'.

Problem 102. Given are two spiral similarities

$$W_1(S_1,\theta_1,\mu_1) \text{ and } W_2(S_2,\theta_2,\mu_2).$$

Determine the centre, angle of rotation, and scale factor of the spiral similarity $W = W_2W_1$.

To solve this problem we construct two pairs of corresponding points for W; the problem then reduces to Problem 100.

The construction is particularly simple if we select A to be the point S_1 and B to be the point which is mapped onto S_2 by the transformation W_1. We have: $\theta = \theta_1+\theta_2$, $\mu = \mu_1\mu_2$.

Problem 103. Construct a cyclic quadrilateral given the lengths of the four sides.

Consider a spiral similarity with centre A which maps B onto D. The image C' of C lies on the line through C and D, since opposite angles of the quadrangle are supplementary (see Figure 78). For this spiral similarity we have $\theta = \alpha$ and $\mu = d/a$. If we start the construction by drawing side c, we can first find C', using $b' = b.d/a$.

We now have two geometric loci for A; we have $AD = d$, and also $AC':AC = d:a$ (Apollonius's circle).

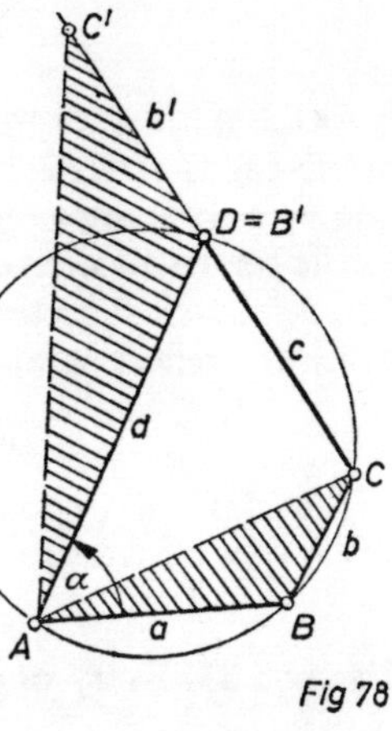

Fig 78

Problem 104. AB is a given line segment and g an arbitrary line through A. If we map AB by all possible spiral similarities with a given centre S which leave the image of A on the line g, show that the geometric locus of B' is a line s. What relation exists between the two lines g and s?

Consider the different images of AB and interpret the correspondence between starting point and end-point of these line segments as a mapping.

OPPOSITE SIMILARITIES

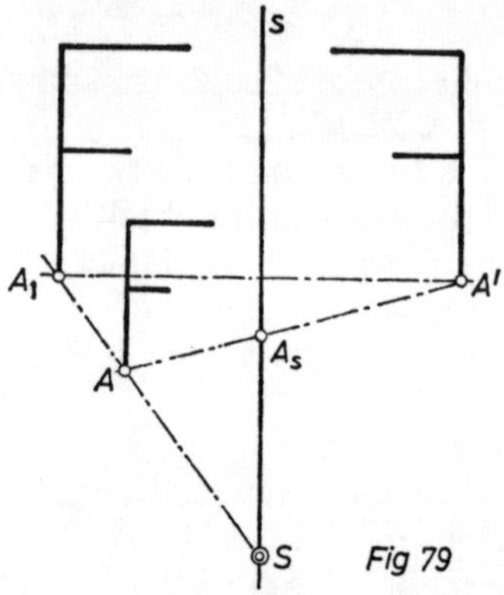

Fig 79

As the simplest example of an opposite similarity we consider the so-called *stretch-reflection*. We obtain this type of translation by combining a reflection M_s with an enlargement E which has its centre on s. As can be deduced immediately from Figure 79, the stretch-reflection Z does not depend upon the order in which the reflection and the enlargement are carried out:

$$Z = EM_s = M_sE.$$

The class of opposite similarities is also dominated by a single type of transformation:

Theorem 17. Every opposite similarity is a stretch-reflection.

The proof is similar to the corresponding one for direct similarities. We refer again to Figure 75 and the transformations defined there. If, in addition, we denote the line through A' and B' by r, we can represent Ω^* by the following product:

$$\Omega^* = EM_rM_qM_p = EK^*.$$

K^* is an opposite isometry. For the further reduction of Ω^* we consider Figure 80 which illustrates the position of the three lines p, q, r and the centre S.

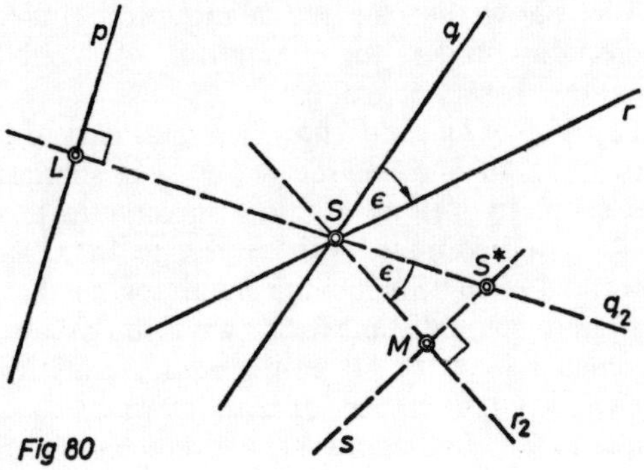

Fig 80

From this figure we deduce

$$\Omega^* = EM_rM_qM_p = EM_{r_2}(M_{q_2}M_p) = M_{r_2}EH_L.$$

The transformations M_{r_2} and E commute since S lies on r_2. $EH_L = E^*$ is again an enlargement with centre S^* on q_2. If we now introduce the perpendicular s to r_2 through S^*, we obtain

$$\Omega^* = M_{r_2}EH_L = M_{r_2}E^* = (M_{r_2}M_s)(M_sE^*) = H_ME^*M_s.$$

Here we have used the fact that E^* and M_s commute since S^* lies on s. $E\dagger = H_ME^*$ is an enlargement with centre $S\dagger$ on s. We have now obtained the following representation for Ω^*:

$$\Omega^* = E\dagger M_s.$$

This is a stretch-reflection, since $S\dagger$ lies on s.

The essential elements of a stretch-reflection are the axis of reflection s, the centre of enlargement S on s, and the scale factor μ.

Problem 105. The two pairs of points A, A' and B, B' are given. Describe the stretch-reflection Z which maps A onto A' and B onto B'.

The scale factor μ is given by $A'B'/AB$. It can be seen from Figure 79 that the axis s divides the line segment AA' in the ration $1:\mu$. Therefore we can immediately construct two points of s.

Problem 106. Show that the set of all spiral similarities and stretch-reflections under the operation of combination of transformations forms a group $\mathfrak{S}^*$.

$\mathfrak{S}^*$ is the *group of all similarities.* The geometry of this group, in the sense of Klein, is called the geometry of similarity.

To this geometry belong all those geometric properties of figures which are invariants with respect to $\mathfrak{S}^*$. Examples are the orthocentre of a triangle, the mediator as the geometric locus of all points equidistant from two given points, the circle as the geometric locus of all points equidistant from a given point. We can say that circles form an invariant class of curves with respect to $\mathfrak{S}^*$. Pythagoras's Theorem also belongs to the geometry of similarity, for if we have $a^2+b^2 = c^2$ for a triangle, the same is true for the image triangle.

Problem 107. The spiral similarities form a subgroup $\mathfrak{S}$ of $\mathfrak{S}^*$. Why do the stretch-reflections fail to form a subgroup?

Problem 108. Determine the group $\mathfrak{S}_F$ of all similarities leaving the pattern in Figure 70 invariant. List also some subgroups of $\mathfrak{S}_F$.

Problem 109. What kind of transformation is $\Psi K \Psi^{-1}$ if $K \in \mathfrak{K}$ and $\Psi \in \mathfrak{S}^*$?
What do we obtain when K is:
(a) a reflection,
(b) a half-turn,
(c) a translation,
(d) a rotation,
(e) a glide-reflection?

Definition. If a geometric figure F can be mapped onto a figure F' by a transformation $\Psi \in \mathfrak{S}^*$, then we say that F and F' are similar figures.

Problem 110. Show that the relation of similarity defined above is an equivalence relation.

Problem 111. A triangle ABC is given. Corresponding to each side construct a vector which is at right-angles to the side, is twice as long as the side, and which points outwards from the triangle. Prove that the vector sum of the three vectors is zero.

Problem 112. *A*, *B*, *C*, *D* are the vertices of a square (described in an anticlockwise direction). Consider the three spiral similarities

$$W_1(A, 45°, \sqrt{2}),$$
$$W_2(B, 45°, \sqrt{2}),$$
$$W_3(C, 90°, \tfrac{1}{2}).$$

What transformation is $W_3 W_2 W_1$?

Problem 113. What kind of transformation is Ψ^2 if Ψ is a stretch-reflection?

9

AFFINE TRANSFORMATIONS

The transformations we have discussed so far were really elementary geometry in a new guise. Now we come to the first example of a mapping which does not belong to the framework of elementary geometry. We enter at the same time a field of geometry of rather more recent origin; affine transformations were first introduced in 1748 by Leonhard Euler (1707-1783) in his analysis of the infinite.*

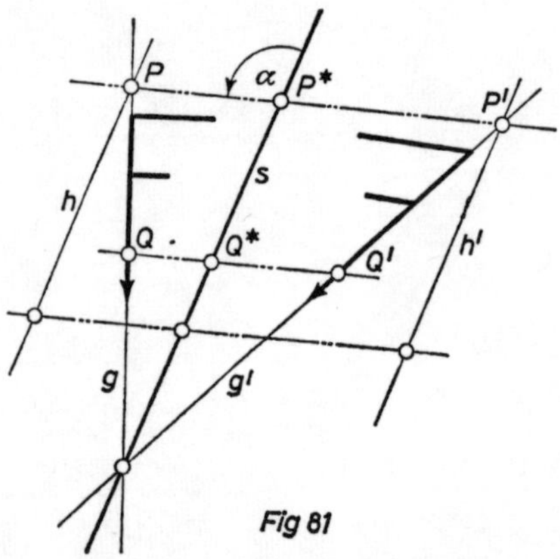

Fig 81

Let us select a line s in the plane and a direction given by the angle α it makes with s. We also choose a real number μ, positive or negative but not zero.

We can now define a mapping of the plane by the following law of correspondence:

The lines through pairs of corresponding points P, P' are parallel to the given direction.

* Euler L.: *Introductio in analysin infinitorum.* Tomus secundus. Cap XVIII, De similitudine et affinitate linearum curvarum. Opera omnia 1/9.

For every pair of points P, P′ we have

$$\frac{P'P^*}{PP^*} = \mu,$$

where P^* is the intersection of the line PP′ with s.

This transformation is called a *perspective affinity*†; *s* is the *axis of affinity*, the given direction is called the *direction of affinity*, and μ is called the *scale factor of the affinity*.

When we wish to describe the transformation fully we shall use the symbol $\Phi(s, \alpha, \mu)$.

An important special case of a perspective affinity is reflection in a line, for

$$M_s = \Phi(s, 90°, -1).$$

Perspective affinities for which $\alpha = 90°$ are called *normal affinities*.

PROPERTIES OF PERSPECTIVE AFFINITIES

If we are given a point *P* and its image *P′* under a perspective affinity with axis *s*, then further pairs of corresponding points can easily be constructed. We can use the construction shown in Figure 81 to ensure that

$$\frac{Q'Q^*}{QQ^*} = \frac{P'P^*}{PP^*} = \mu.$$

If *Q* moves along the line *g*, then *Q′* moves along *g′* (in our construction only the parallel to the direction of affinity moves). Hence, *g′* is the image of *g* under the affinity.

If *h* is parallel to *s*, then the image points of *h* lie on a parallel line *h′*. This is a consequence of the fact that if *P* moves along the line *h*, then the distance PP^* remains constant; hence $P'P^*$ is constant, too.

1. A perspective affinity is a line-preserving transformation. Corresponding lines intersect on the axis of affinity.

The line *s* is a fixed line; in fact, all points of *s* are fixed points. The lines parallel to the direction of affinity are also fixed lines, but, unlike *s*, they are not pointwise fixed.

† Or axial stretching.

The verification of the following properties offers no particular difficulties; accordingly no detailed explanation is necessary.

2. A perspective affinity maps parallel lines onto parallel lines.

3. The transformation preserves ratios of division; the ratios of distances of three points on a line g are equal to the corresponding ratios for the image points on g'.

4. The ratio of the area of a polygon to its image under a perspective affinity is $1:\mu$.*

5. A perspective affinity is a one-one mapping. The inverse affinity has the same axis and direction but has scale factor $\mu' = 1/\mu$.

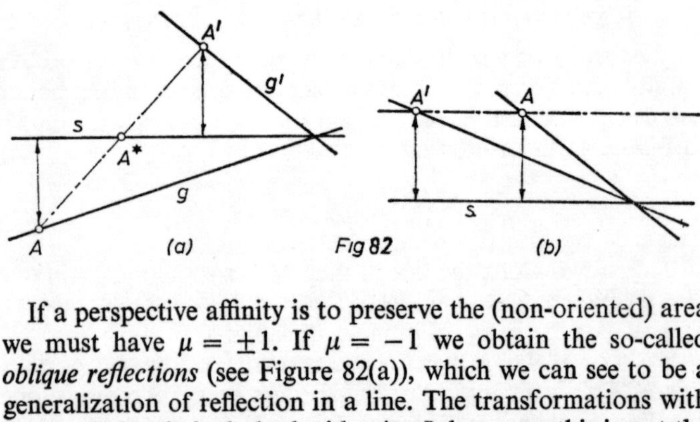

Fig 82

If a perspective affinity is to preserve the (non-oriented) area we must have $\mu = \pm 1$. If $\mu = -1$ we obtain the so-called *oblique reflections* (see Figure 82(a)), which we can see to be a generalization of reflection in a line. The transformations with $\mu = 1$ obviously include the identity I; however, this is not the only affinity with this property. If we note that the scale factor can also be expressed in terms of the oriented distances of corresponding points A and A' from s, we deduce that if $\mu = 1$ these distances are equal. If $\Phi \neq I$, then the direction of affinity must be parallel to s. In this case we speak of a *shear* with the axis s (see Figure 82(b)).

* We are here considering orientated areas. The ratio of the areas is positive or negative according to whether the original and image polygons have the same orientation or not.

If $\alpha = 0$, μ can no longer be chosen arbitrarily. μ is then always $+1$. For a shear α and μ are not independent, and as a consequence the transformation is not completely determined by s, α and μ. A shear is a degenerate type of perspective affinity.

As parallelism is invariant, a square is mapped by a perspective affinity onto a parallelogram. A given quadrangle can only be mapped onto a square by a perspective affinity if its opposite sides are parallel. The following problem shows that this condition is not only necessary but is also sufficient.

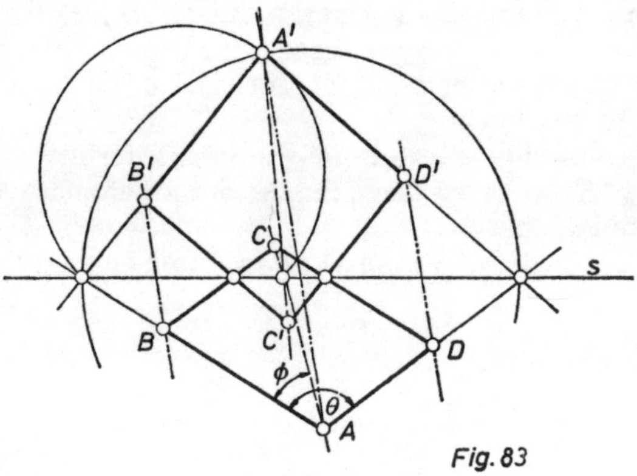

Fig. 83

Problem 114. Find a perspective affinity with given axis s which maps a given parallelogram $ABCD$ onto a square.

The image of a parallelogram under a perspective affinity is always another parallelogram, since parallel lines have parallel images. Hence, the parallelograms form an invariant class of quadrangles with respect to the perspective affinities. The image parallelogram is a square if the angle θ' between two sides is 90° and the angle ϕ' between a side and a diagonal is 45°. The conditions

$$\theta \to \theta' = 90° \text{ and } \phi \to \phi' = 45°$$

define two geometric loci for A'. Their intersection is A'. Once we have a pair of corresponding points we can, of course, easily construct the transformation. The complete geometric loci have a second point of intersection which is the image of A' under reflection in s. If we ask for the transformation, the problem has two solutions. The two squares obtained are, however, congruent and we shall later prove this.

Among the numerous properties which characterize quadrangles, only those which characterize parallelograms are invariant under perspective affinities. Examples are the properties that opposite sides are parallel, or that the diagonals bisect each other. In general, a perspective affinity will not preserve angles.

Problem 115. Show that a hexagon can be mapped by a perspective affinity onto a regular hexagon if and only if its diagonals are concurrent and pairs of opposite sides of the hexagon are parallel to a diagonal.

The two conditions are certainly necessary, for they are satisfied by a regular hexagon and they are invariant under perspective affinities.

We can obtain a hexagon satisfying these conditions in the

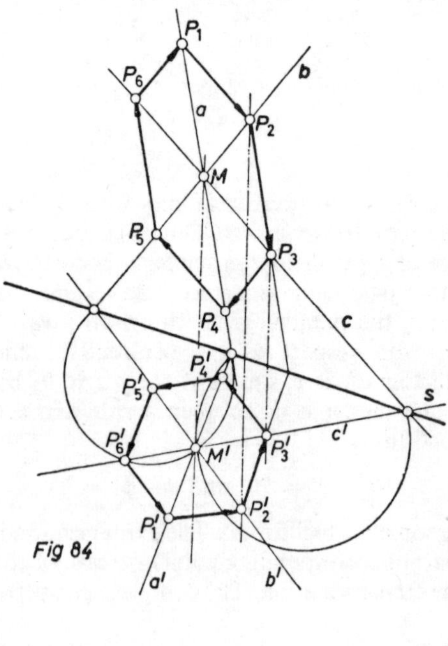

Fig 84

following way (see Figure 84). We start with the three diagonals a, b, c intersecting in a point M. We choose a point P_1 on a and draw through it a line parallel to c; this determines P_2 on b. Then draw a line parallel to a to obtain P_3, etc. Finally we obtain P_6. The parallel to b through P_6 passes through P_1 and completes the hexagon. This follows from the relation

$$P_1P_2 = MP_3 = P_4P_5 = MP_6.$$

We can now prescribe the axis of affinity s in an arbitrary manner.

If we determine the affinity in such a way that a, b, c are mapped onto three lines intersecting each other at angles of 60°, then the image of $P_1P_2 \ldots P_6$ will be a regular hexagon, since the six triangles which make up the image hexagon will be equilateral.

Problem 116. Given a triangle ABC, a line s and a point S', construct a perspective affinity having s as its axis and such that S' is the centroid of the triangle $A'B'C'$.

The position of the centroid of a triangle is determined by certain ratios of line segments. Since such ratios are invariants under perspective affinities, it follows that the image of the centroid of ABC is the centroid of the image triangle $A'B'C'$. The notion of a centroid is invariant under perspective affinities.

We can construct the centroid S of the given triangle ABC. S and S' are then corresponding points which determine the transformation.

The centroid S of a quadrangle $ABCD$ can be found by two different decompositions into triangles (see Figure 85). This combined construction is also affine, that is, it is built up using properties which are all invariant under perspective affinities. The affine image of the construction coincides with the corresponding construction for the affine image of the quadrangle.

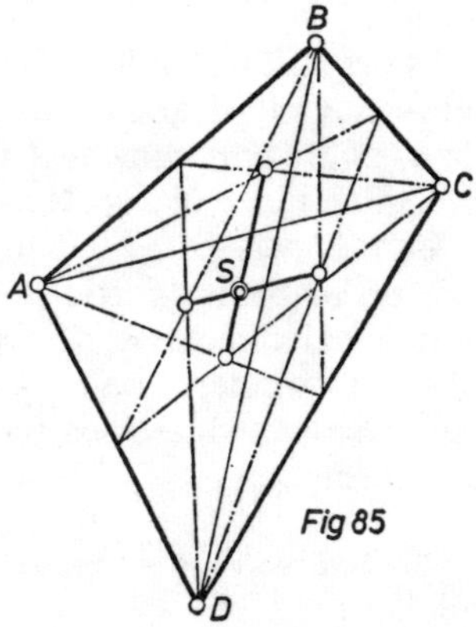

Fig 85

Problem 117. Verify the construction of F. Wittenbauer* for the centroid of a quadrangle. This construction is shown in Figure 86 and is also invariant under affine transformations. The sides of the quadrangle are divided into three equal parts and a parallelogram is then obtained by drawing lines through pairs of points of trisection adjoining a vertex. The sides of this parallelogram are parallel to the diagonals of the given quadrangle and the diagonals of the parallelogram intersect in the centroid of the quadrangle.

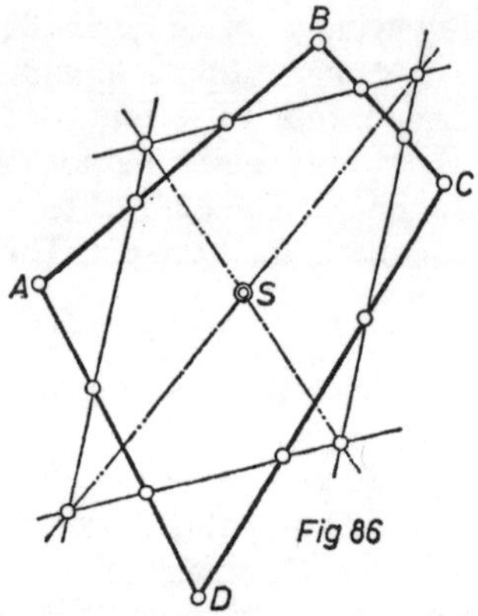

Fig 86

Wittenbauer's construction can be reduced to the construction shown in Figure 85 by purely geometric means, that is, without calculation.

Problem 118. Give a construction for finding the centroid of a pentagon.

Problem 119. Given are the axis of a perspective affinity and a pair of corresponding points A and A'. Construct two orthogonal lines u and v which intersect at A and which have orthogonal images.

The problem is solved by constructing a circle which passes through A and A' and has its centre M on s. M lies on the mediator m of the line segment AA'. Figure 87 is based on a perspective affinity having a scale factor $\mu > 0$.

Since a perspective affinity preserves parallelism, there are two orthogonal directions which are always mapped onto orthogonal directions. We always obtain this same pair of directions whatever pair of corresponding points we use. We call these two directions the *invariant right-angle pair* of the transformation.

* See Strubecker, K., *Einführung in die höhere Mathematik.* Vol. 1, p. 403, Munich, 1956.

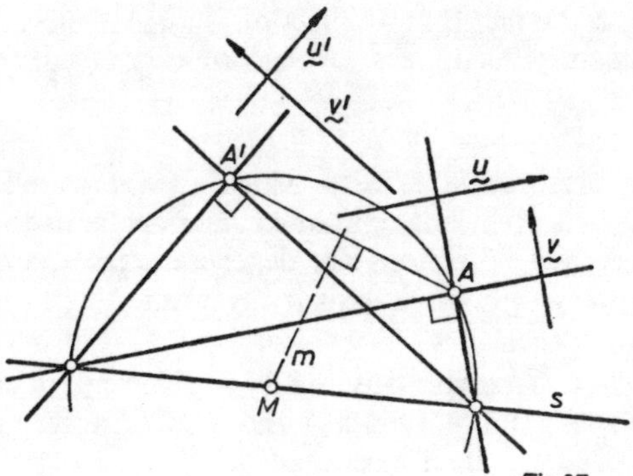

Fig 87

This construction runs into difficulties if the direction of affinity is at right-angles to the axis, that is, for normal affinities.

Consider first the case $\mu \neq -1$, that is, the transformation is not a reflection. Then m is parallel to s but different from s (see Figure 88). The circle through AA' now becomes a straight line through these points. The invariant right-angle pair exists in this case too; one direction is parallel to, the other orthogonal to, the axis of affinity.

For a reflection ($\mu = -1$) m and s coincide; the point of intersection is, therefore, indeterminate (see Figure 89). Every point of s can be taken as the centre of a circle passing through A and A'. Hence, every right-angle is invariant. The result

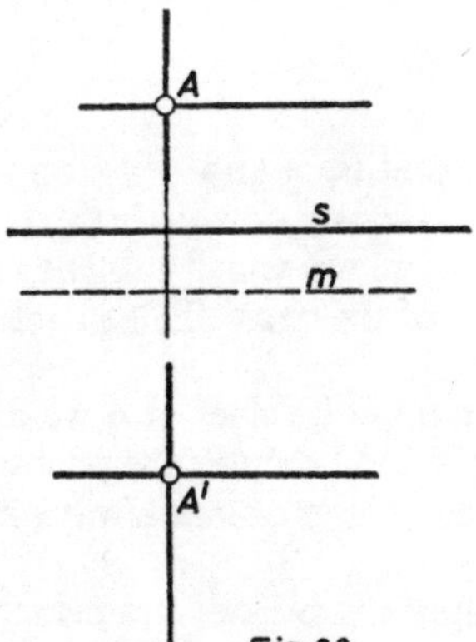

Fig. 88

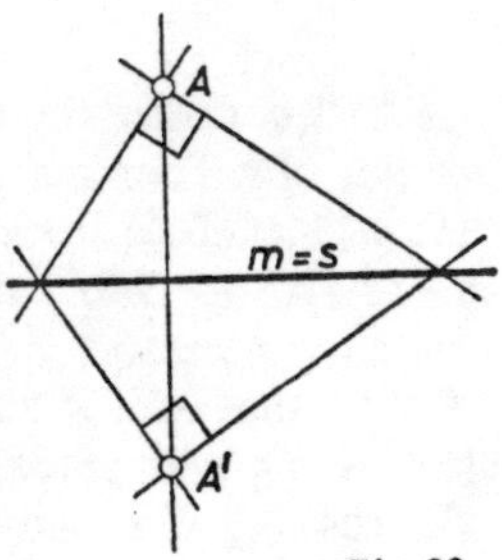

Fig. 89

agrees with the fact that a reflection is an isometry.

We can sum this up as a further property of our transformations:

6. Every perspective affinity which is not a reflection has exactly one invariant right-angle pair. As far as this property is concerned reflections are degenerate cases; under reflections every right-angle pair is invariant.

Problem 120. A perspective affinity is given by its axis s and a pair of corresponding points A and A'. Construct an invariant 60°-pair of lines which meet at A.

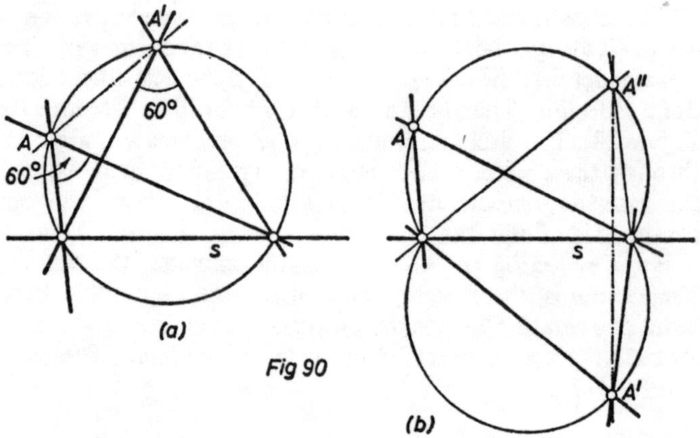

Fig 90

We first consider the case $\mu>0$, that is, A and A' lie on the same side of s. Then our problem is to construct a circle through A and A' such that the axis s cuts off an arc which subtends an angle of 120° (or 240°) at the centre of the circle. This problem has already been solved in Problem 77.

If $\mu<0$, that is, if A and A' lie on opposite sides of s, we first reflect A' in s. This leads to a point A'' and reduces the problem to the case $\mu>0$ already considered. The problem always has two solutions.

In the solution for $\mu<0$ there appears, besides the perspective affinity Φ, the reflection M_s. In order to find the invariant

60°-pair for the transformation Φ, we first determine the corresponding pair for the mapping $M_s\Phi$. This is again a perspective affinity with axis s.

The importance of perspective affinities lies in their connection with the parallel projection. For this reason construction problems on perspective affinities can be found in many collections of problems in descriptive geometry. Therefore we restrict ourselves here to considering certain problems which bring out new aspects.

THE GROUP PROPERTIES OF PERSPECTIVE AFFINITIES

The remark at the end of Problem 120 leads us to the conjecture that the perspective affinities with a given axis form a group. In order to check this we shall use methods of analytic geometry.

We consider first a perspective affinity $\Phi(s, \alpha, \mu)$ and set up a rectangular coordinate system as shown in Figure 91. The x-axis is taken to coincide with the axis of affinity s. Our transformation Φ, which maps A onto A', is then characterized by the equations:

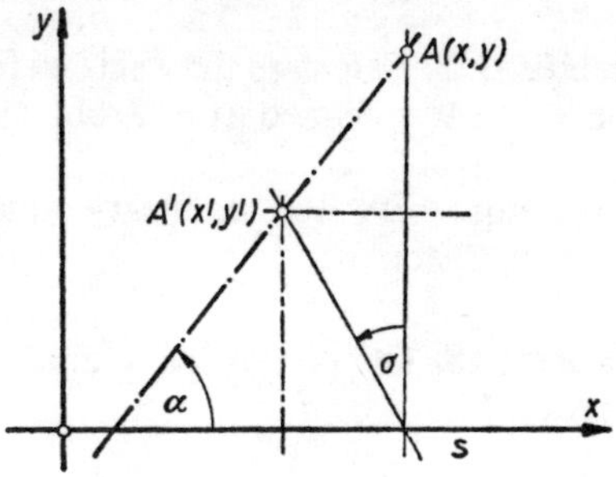

Fig 91

$$x' = x+(\mu-1)\cot\alpha\, y,$$
$$y' = \mu y.$$

However, we have seen that shears cannot be characterized by the parameters α and μ. In order to find a standardized representation for all perspective affinities we have to look for more suitable parameters.

Since the transformation Φ preserves parallelism, the angle between a, the perpendicular from A to s, and its image line a' is independent of the choice of A. Corresponding to every perspective affinity Φ there is a well-defined angle σ. Now we have

$$\tan \sigma = \frac{x-x'}{y'} = \frac{1-\mu}{\mu \tan \alpha}$$

or

$$(\mu-1) \cot \alpha = -\mu \tan \sigma.$$

We now replace α in our transformation equations by the parameter σ. The equations can then be written:

$$x' = x-\mu \tan \sigma\, y,$$
$$y' = \mu y,$$

and it is easy to see that these equations are also valid for shears. Tan σ always has a finite value.*

Problem 121. A perspective affinity Φ has axis s, angle $\sigma = 45°$, and scale factor $\mu = \frac{1}{3}$. Construct a pair of corresponding points.

Problem 122. Calculate the angle σ' for the inverse transformation Φ^{-1} (Φ is defined as in Problem 121).

We now have the necessary analytic tools to prove the following theorem:

Theorem 18. The perspective affinities with a given axis s form a group $\mathfrak{Q}_s$.

Let Φ_1 and Φ_2 be two perspective affinities having the same axis s. We use the notation (see Figure 92)

$$A(x,y) \xrightarrow[\Phi_1]{} A'(x',y') \xrightarrow[\Phi_2]{} A''(x'',y'').$$

Then the equations of the transformations are

$$\Phi_1 \begin{cases} x' = x-\mu_1 \tan \sigma_1\, y, \\ y' = \mu_1 y, \end{cases} \qquad \Phi_2 \begin{cases} x'' = x'-\mu_2 \tan \sigma_2\, y', \\ y'' = \mu_2 y'. \end{cases}$$

The geometric composition of Φ_1 and Φ_2 so as to form the new transformation $\Phi = \Phi_2\Phi_1$ corresponds to the algebraic

* Note that α and σ are directed angles.

substitution of the equations for Φ_1 into those for Φ_2. We obtain

$$\begin{aligned} x'' &= x-\mu_1 \tan \sigma_1\, y-\mu_1\mu_2 \tan \sigma_2\, y \\ &= x-(\mu_1 \tan \sigma_1+\mu_1\mu_2 \tan \sigma_2)y, \\ y'' &= \mu_1\mu_2 y. \end{aligned}$$

These equations, too, have the structure of transformation equations for a perspective affinity with axis s. If we write

$$\begin{aligned} x'' &= x-\mu \tan \sigma\, y, \\ y'' &= \mu\, y, \end{aligned}$$

then we obtain by comparison,

$$\begin{aligned} \mu &= \mu_1\mu_2, \\ \mu \tan \sigma &= \mu_1 \tan \sigma_1+\mu_1\mu_2 \tan \sigma_2. \end{aligned}$$

This implies the following rules of composition for the scale factors and angles:

$$\Phi = \Phi_2\Phi_1 \Rightarrow \begin{cases} \mu = \mu_1\mu_2 \\ \tan \sigma = 1/\mu_2 \tan \sigma_1+\tan \sigma_2. \end{cases}$$

Hence, the mapping obtained by combining two perspective affinities with axis s is again a perspective affinity with axis s. The verification of the remaining group postulates is trivial.

Corresponding to every line s there exists a group $\mathfrak{Q}_s$. This fact is expressed by using the suffix s in the symbol for the group.

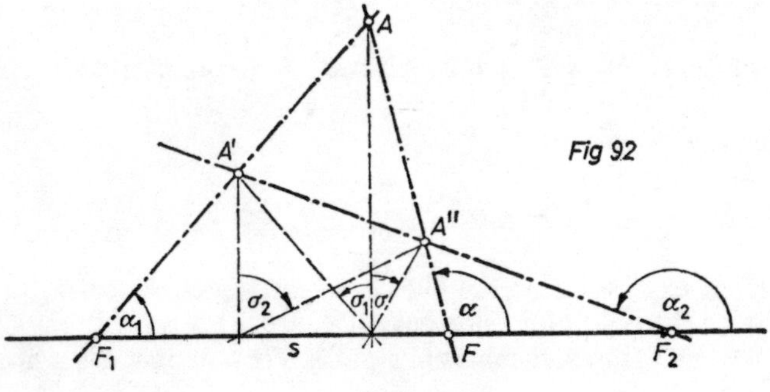

Fig 92

The group $\mathfrak{Q}_s$ is not commutative. This can be seen immediately from the rule for obtaining the angle of the product transformation, since the formula for σ is not symmetric in the pairs $(\mu_1, \tan \sigma_1)$ and $(\mu_2, \tan \sigma_2)$.

Problem 123. Show that in the group $\mathfrak{Q}_s$ we have the following rule for obtaining the direction of affinity of the product transformation:

$$\tan \alpha = \frac{(1-\mu_1\mu_2)\tan \alpha_1 \tan \alpha_2}{(1-\mu_1)\tan \alpha_2+\mu_1(1-\mu_2)\tan \alpha_1}.$$

Problem 124. Prove the theorem of Menelaus using transformations belonging to the group $\mathfrak{Q}_s$ (cf. Problem 87).

We are now in a position to settle a question which arose in connection with Problem 114. Then we constructed an affinity with a given axis s which mapped a parallelogram onto a square. We found that there was a second transformation having this property and that

$$\Phi_2 = M_s\Phi_1.$$

But from this it follows at once that the two squares obtained are congruent (and are symmetrically placed with respect to the axis).

Problem 125. Show that two transformations $\Phi_1, \Phi_2 \in \mathfrak{Q}_s$ commute if, and only if, their directions of affinity coincide $(\alpha_1 = \alpha_2)$.

From the rules of composition we found

$$\Phi_2\Phi_1 = \Phi_1\Phi_2 \Leftrightarrow \frac{1}{\mu_2}\tan \sigma_1+\tan \sigma_2 = \frac{1}{\mu_1}\tan \sigma_2+\tan \sigma_1.$$

This can be written

$$\frac{\mu_1}{1-\mu_1}\tan \sigma_1 = \frac{\mu_2}{1-\mu_2}\tan \sigma_2.$$

But the expression on the left-hand side represents $\cot \alpha_1$ and that on the right-hand side $\cot \alpha_2$, hence, $\alpha_1 = \alpha_2$.

We can easily find subgroups of $\mathfrak{Q}_s$. We note that s is a fixed line for all $\Phi \in \mathfrak{Q}_s$. By demanding further invariants we obtain subgroups of $\mathfrak{Q}_s$.

If we demand that a certain direction should be an invariant, we obtain the subgroup $\mathfrak{Q}_{s(\alpha)}$ of all the transformations having the same direction of affinity (given by the angle α). It follows from Problem 123 that $\mathfrak{Q}_{s(\alpha)}$ is a commutative group; the composition of mappings in the group being given by the relation $\mu = \mu_1\mu_2$ obtained above.

Another subgroup $\mathfrak{Q}_s' \subset \mathfrak{Q}_s$ can be obtained by demanding the invariance of the measure of area. $\mathfrak{Q}_s'$ contains the perspective affinities with $\mu = \pm 1$, that is, shears and oblique reflections. The shears alone form a group $\mathfrak{Q}_s'' \subset \mathfrak{Q}'_s$.

Problem 126. Show that in the group $\mathfrak{Q}_s''$ the composition of transformations can be described by the relation

$$\tan \sigma = \tan \sigma_1 + \tan \sigma_2.$$

Illustrate this result diagrammatically..

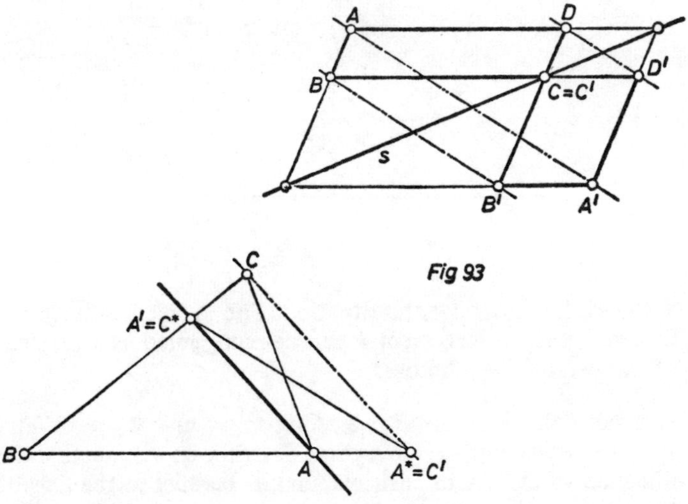

Fig 93

Problem 127. Interpret the two constructions shown in Figure 93, in which the two image figures have the same area as the original figures, in terms of mappings belonging to $\mathfrak{Q}_s$.

Problem 128. Show that shears having the same axis s and such that $\tan \sigma = na$ where n is an integer and a a constant, form a group. Try to give a geometric figure which is invariant with respect to this group (cf. Figure 70).

The product of perspective affinities having different axes is, in general, not a perspective affinity. For example, the product of two reflections is a rotation or a translation. These are mappings having either one fixed point or none at all and, therefore, cannot be perspective affinities.

Problem 129. Two perspective affinities Φ_1 and Φ_2 have axes which intersect in a point S. The direction of affinity of each mapping is parallel to the axis of the other, and we have $\mu_1 = \mu_2 = \mu$. Show that $\Phi_2\Phi_1$ is the enlargement $E(S,\mu)$ and that the two transformations Φ_1 and Φ_2 commute.

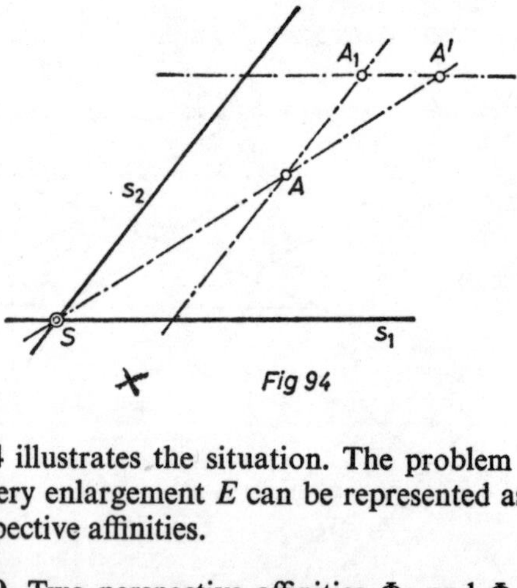

Fig 94

Figure 94 illustrates the situation. The problem reveals the fact that every enlargement E can be represented as a product of two perspective affinities.

Problem 130. Two perspective affinities Φ_1 and Φ_2 have axes s_1 and s_2 which intersect in a point S. Again we assume that the direction of affinity of each mapping is parallel to the axis of the other, but now we suppose that $\mu_1\mu_2 = 1$.

(a) Show that $\Phi_2\Phi_1$ is a transformation which preserves lines and area, and that S is a fixed point of the transformation.

(b) Let A be a point on s_1 and B a point on s_2. Show that the lines through the pairs A, B' $(= \Phi_2\Phi_1(B))$ and B, A' $(= \Phi_2\Phi_1(A))$ are parallel.

(c) Show that $\Phi_2\Phi_1 = \Phi_1\Phi_2$.

Problem 131. Φ_1 and Φ_2 are two given perspective affinities satisfying the conditions of Problem 130. Setting $\mu_1 = \lambda$, we see that $\mu_2 = 1/\lambda$, and that we can write

$$\Phi_2\Phi_1 = \Phi(\lambda).$$

(a) Show that the transformations $\Phi(\lambda)$ (for all $\lambda \neq 0$) with given axes s_1 and s_2 form a commutative group $\mathfrak{Q}(s_1, s_2)$.

(b) Translate the group relation

$$\Phi(\lambda_2\lambda_1) = \Phi(\lambda_2)\Phi(\lambda_1)$$

into geometric language. (Use the result of Problem 130(b)—the Pappus-Pascal configuration.)

Problem 132. Show that hyperbolae with asymptotes s_1 and s_2 are invariant under transformations of the group $\mathfrak{Q}(s_1, s_2)$.†

If Φ_1 and Φ_2 are two arbitrary perspective affinities, then the transformation $\Phi_2\Phi_1$ is obviously a mapping which preserves lines, parallelism and ratios of division. These properties of Φ_1 and Φ_2 are not lost by composition. We have met other transformations with these properties, for example, the elements of the groups $\mathfrak{R}$ and $\mathfrak{S}^*$.

Definition. Every finite product of perspective affinities is called a *general affine transformation* or, for short, an *affinity*.

It follows from the definition that affinities are transformations which preserve lines, parallelism and the ratios of division. They form a group $\mathfrak{Q}$, the full affine group. The groups $\mathfrak{Q}_s$ are subgroups of $\mathfrak{Q}$. Moreover, $\mathfrak{R}$ and $\mathfrak{S}^*$ are also subgroups of $\mathfrak{Q}$, since we have seen that the reflections, which generate $\mathfrak{R}$, are particular perspective affinities, and Problem 129 showed that

† This property is used in the geometric introduction of the natural logarithm. See, for example, Van der Waerden B. L., *Die Einführung des Logarithmus im Schulunterricht*. El. Math. 12, 1957.

every enlargement could be obtained as the product of two perspective affinities.

Problem 133. Given are two triangles *ABC* and *A'B'C'*. Show that there exist a perspective affinity Φ and a spiral similarity Ω such that the transformation ΩΦ maps the triangle *ABC* onto the triangle *A'B'C'*.

Take, for example, the spiral similarity which maps the line segment *AB* onto the segment *A'B'*. Then it is easy to find a perspective affinity Φ such that ΩΦ has the required property. The reader will easily work this out with the aid of a simple drawing.

The transformation ΩΦ which we have just constructed is an affinity. Hence, there always exists an affinity mapping a given triangle *ABC* onto a second given triangle *A'B'C'*, and there exists only one such affinity as we shall proceed to show. If we want to construct the image of an arbitrary point *P*, we can do this in the following way. We draw lines through *P* parallel to *AC* and *AB*. Let these lines intersect *AB* and *AC* in the points P_1 and P_2 respectively. Since ratios of division are invariant we can immediately construct the images P_1' and P_2' on the sides *A'B'* and *A'C'* of the image triangle. If we then draw lines parallel to *A'B'* and *A'C'* through these points, we find *P'*, the image point of *P*. Hence, the image of any point, and therefore the affinity, is uniquely determined by the triangles *ABC* and *A'B'C'*. There can be only one such affinity. The decomposition into a spiral similarity and a perspective affinity is, however, not unique.

The group 𝔄 has finite subgroups as well. If we ask, for example, for the affine transformations which leave a given triangle *ABC* invariant, then we see that any such transformation produces a permutation of the three vertices. Since there are only six permutations, it follows that there are only six affine transformations of the triangle onto itself, and that these six elements form a group. We shall follow up this example by looking in more detail at the affinities which map a given parallelogram *ABCD* onto itself. Every such affinity again results in a permutation of the vertices. Since the affinity is determined by the images *A'*, *B'*, *C'* of the points *A*, *B*, *C*, we can characterize the affinity by giving the positions of A', B', C' on the parallelogram. This choice is not arbitrary, for D has to be mapped onto a vertex as well. This will only happen if A', B', C' are (in this order) adjoining vertices of the parallelogram. There are eight possibilities for this. Four of these preserve the orientation, and four reverse the orientation of the parallelogram. There are, therefore, eight affinities which leave the parallelogram invariant. They form a group $\mathfrak{Q}_8$ and the eight mappings can be described as follows (see Figure 95):

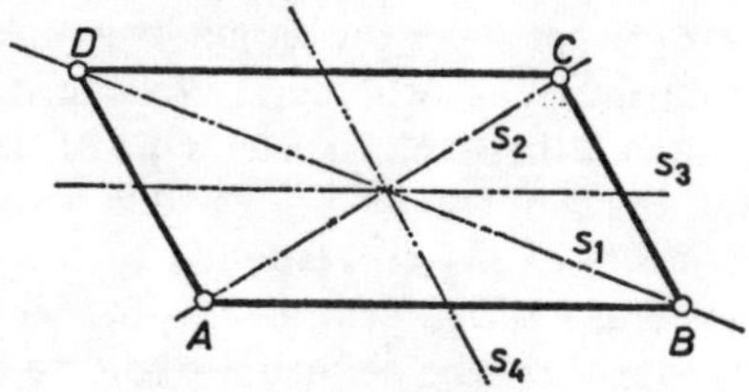

Fig 95

- I identity transformation
- Φ_1 affinity moving the vertices round one place in an anti-clockwise direction
- Φ_2 affinity moving the vertices round two places in an anti-clockwise direction
- Φ_3 affinity moving the vertices round three places in an anti-clockwise direction
- Φ_1' oblique reflection with axis s_1
- Φ_2' oblique reflection with axis s_2
- Φ_3' oblique reflection with axis s_3
- Φ_4' oblique reflection with axis s_4.

The group table for these transformations is

	I	Φ_1	Φ_2	Φ_3	Φ_1'	Φ_2'	Φ_3'	Φ_4'
I	I	Φ_1	Φ_2	Φ_3	Φ_1'	Φ_2'	Φ_3'	Φ_4'
Φ_1	Φ_1	Φ_2	Φ_3	I	Φ_3'	Φ_4'	Φ_2'	Φ_1'
Φ_2	Φ_2	Φ_3	I	Φ_1	Φ_2'	Φ_1'	Φ_4'	Φ_3'
Φ_3	Φ_3	I	Φ_1	Φ_2	Φ_4'	Φ_3'	Φ_1'	Φ_2'
Φ_1'	Φ_1'	Φ_4'	Φ_2'	Φ_3'	I	Φ_2	Φ_3	Φ_1
Φ_2'	Φ_2'	Φ_3'	Φ_1'	Φ_4'	Φ_2	I	Φ_1	Φ_3
Φ_3'	Φ_3'	Φ_1'	Φ_4'	Φ_2'	Φ_1	Φ_3	I	Φ_2
Φ_4'	Φ_4'	Φ_2'	Φ_3'	Φ_1'	Φ_3	Φ_1	Φ_2	I

If we compare this table with the group table for the isometries which map a given square onto itself, we see that the two groups have the same structure although they originated from different problems. We can establish a one-one correspondence between the elements of the group $\mathfrak{G}_8$ for the square and the elements of $\mathfrak{Q}_8$, in such a way that the product of two elements of $\mathfrak{G}_8$ corresponds to the product of corresponding elements in $\mathfrak{Q}_8$. Two groups for which such a one-one correspondence can be defined are said to be *isomorphic*.

In Problem 114 we showed that every parallelogram can be mapped onto a square by some affinity. If we denote this affinity by Ψ, then we have the following relations between the elements of $\mathfrak{G}_8$ and $\mathfrak{Q}_8$:

$$R_j = \Psi\Phi_j\Psi^{-1}; \quad M_j = \Psi\Phi_j'\Psi^{-1},$$

and we have, for example,

$$\begin{aligned} M_3R_1 &= (\Psi\Phi_3'\Psi^{-1})(\Psi\Phi_1\Psi^{-1}) \\ &= \Psi(\Phi_3'\Phi_1)\Psi^{-1}. \end{aligned}$$

This describes the isomorphism between the two groups geometrically. The two problems leading to the groups $\mathfrak{G}_8$ and $\mathfrak{Q}_8$ were not, therefore, basically different. The transformations Φ_1, Φ_2, Φ_3 are rotations deformed by an affinity, and Φ_1', Φ_2', Φ_3', Φ_4' are reflections which have been deformed.

Another interpretation of the isomorphism springs from the fact that the groups $\mathfrak{G}_8$ and $\mathfrak{Q}_8$ describe the same group of permutations of the vertices *A*, *B*, *C*, *D*.

Problem 134. Show that the perspective affinities with the same direction of affinity form a group.

Problem 135. Show that if an affinity has a pointwise fixed line *s*, then it is a perspective affinity with axis *s*.

Let *A*, *A'* be a pair of corresponding points for the given affinity Φ and suppose that *A* does not lie on *s*. Making use of the fact that affinities preserve ratios of division, we can construct the image point *P'* of any point *P* from *s*, *A* and *A'*. This image is unique; hence it follows that there is only one affine transformation which leaves all points of *s* fixed and maps *A* onto A'. But the perspective affinity with axis s and the pair of corresponding points A, A' is such an affinity.

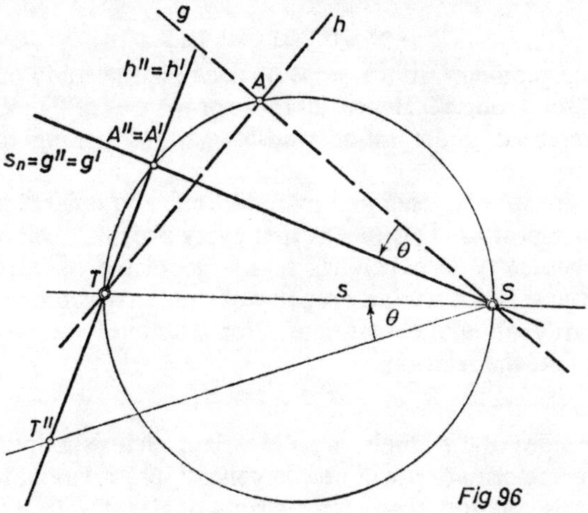

Fig 96

Problem 136. Show that every perspective affinity Φ can be represented as a product of a spiral similarity Ω and a normal affinity Φ_n.

Let Φ be a perspective affinity with the axis s, and let A and A' be a pair of corresponding points under Φ. Construct the invariant right-angle pair at A and A' (see Figure 96). Now we consider a spiral similarity Ω with centre S, angle θ and scale factor $\mu = SA'/SA$.

The images of A, g and h under the transformation Ω are denoted by A'', g'' and h''. By the definition of Ω we have $A' = A''$, $g' = g''$ and $h' = h''$. For the image T'' of T under Ω, we have

$$A'T'' = \mu AT.$$

Now let Φ_n be the normal affinity with axis $s_n = g' = g''$, which maps T'' onto T. Then the transformation $\Phi_n\Omega$ has both S and T as fixed points. Since ratios are invariant it follows that every point on the line s through S and T is also a fixed point. Hence, using the result of Problem 135, $\Phi_n\Omega$ is a perspective affinity with axis s. However, it maps A onto A' and so it must be the given affinity Φ. Hence, $\Phi = \Phi_n \Omega$ which shows that any perspective affinity can be decomposed into a spiral similarity and a normal affinity.†

AFFINE GEOMETRY

Affine geometry, in the sense of Klein, is the study of invariants of the group $\mathfrak{Q}$. Hence, all those properties of figures which are preserved under affine transformations belong to affine geometry.

The group $\mathfrak{S}^*$, generated by reflections and enlargements, is a subgroup of $\mathfrak{Q}$. This means that every property belonging to affine geometry also belongs to the geometry of similarities. The reverse is not true; a property of similarity geometry is not necessarily an affine invariant. For example, we mentioned before that the relation

$$a^2+b^2 = c^2,$$

for the sides of a triangle, is an invariant under similarities. An affine transformation will not, in general, preserve right-angles. Since this relation characterizes right-angles it will not, therefore, be an invariant under $\mathfrak{Q}$. Affine geometry embraces only a subset of the properties which belong to similarity geometry. The theorem of Pythagoras is not one of these; the group of similarities forms an extreme limit for this particular theorem.

However, ratios of areas are conserved by affine transformations. To measure an area means to find out how many times a certain unit area is contained in it. The measure of area is, therefore, based on a relation of the form

$$F_1 = \rho F_2.$$

From the result of Problem 133 we conclude immediately that this relation is preserved by affine transformations. For the affine images we have again

$$F_1' = \rho F_2'.$$

An example of a property which is affine invariant is that the diagonals of a parallelogram divide the figure into four triangles of equal area.

† This decomposition is not unique. We could, for example, start with a spiral similarity with centre T.

The notion of a vector also belongs to affine geometry. This follows from the fact that parallel line segments having equal length are mapped onto image segments which are again parallel and of equal length. Every relation between vectors is an affine invariant; for example, if

$$\boldsymbol{v} = \boldsymbol{a} + 3\boldsymbol{b},$$

then the same relation holds for the image vectors.

Every group defines an equivalence relation between those figures that can be mapped onto each other by transformations of the group. For example, all triangles are equivalent with respect to $\mathfrak{Q}$, for an affine transformation can be found which maps any given triangle onto any other triangle. There is only one class of triangles in affine geometry. In similarity geometry, however, such triangles as the isosceles right-angled triangles form a class by themselves. Parallelograms also form one class in affine geometry, but not trapezia. Two trapezia only belong to the same equivalence class if the ratio of the lengths of the parallel sides is the same. Only then can one be obtained from the other by an affine transformation.

Problem 137. What conditions must be satisfied by a hexagon if it is to belong to the same equivalence class as a given regular hexagon:
(a) with respect to the group $\mathfrak{S}$,
(b) with respect to the group $\mathfrak{Q}$?

Problem 138. Show that two quadrangles belong to the same equivalence class with respect to $\mathfrak{Q}$ if the diagonals in both figures divide each other in the same ratio.

Problem 139. Show that areas of corresponding polygons under a general affine transformation are in a fixed ratio μ.

10

THE AFFINE GEOMETRY OF THE ELLIPSE

We start with the following definition:

Definition. The image of a circle under a perspective affinity is called an *ellipse*.

Since the perspective affinity preserves ratios, every diameter of the circle Γ is mapped onto a diameter of the ellipse Γ'. This fact can be expressed in the language of transformation geometry by writing

$$\Phi H_M \Phi^{-1} = H_{M'}.$$

Corresponding to orthogonal diameters of the circle we obtain what are called *conjugate diameters* of the ellipse (see

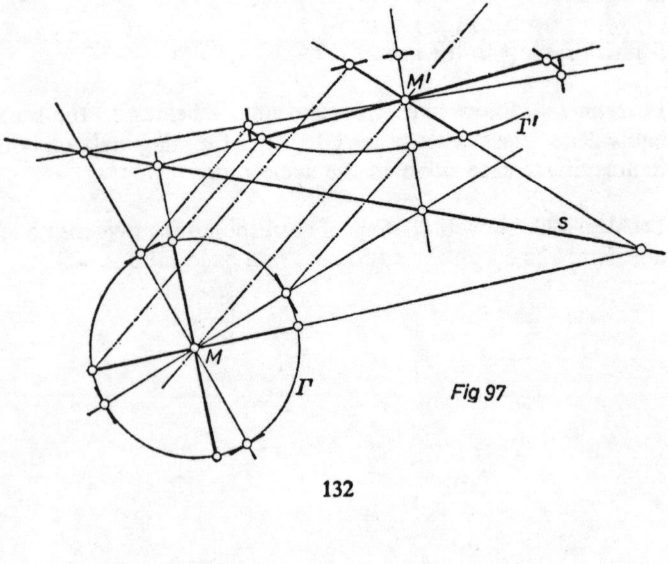

Fig 97

Figure 97). The property of orthogonality is not an affine invariant, but orthogonal diameters of a circle can be characterized by a property which is invariant under affine transformations. This property is that the tangents at the end-points of one diameter are parallel to the other diameter. Conjugate diameters of an ellipse will, therefore, also be characterized by the fact that the tangents at the end-points of one diameter will be parallel to the other diameter. Among these pairs of conjugate diameters there will be one pair which is orthogonal; this pair defines the *axes of the ellipse*. The axes are, therefore, related to the invariant right-angle pair of the affinity.

Problem 140. Construct the axes of an ellipse which is the image of a circle Γ under the perspective affinity Φ.

Problem 141. Show that every ellipse is the image under a normal affinity of the two circles on its axes.

We imagine that the given ellipse is the image of a circle Γ under the perspective affinity Φ. If we construct the invariant right-angle pair for Φ at M and M', then we can reduce the problem to the decomposition of Φ into a spiral similarity Ω and a normal affinity Φ_n, as described in Problem 136. We denote the two normal affinities by Φ_{n1} and Φ_{n2}. If a and b are the lengths of the semi-axes of the ellipse, we have

$$\Phi_{n1}\left(s_1,\ 90^\circ,\ \pm\frac{b}{a}\right) \text{ and } \Phi_{n2}\left(s_2,\ 90^\circ,\ \pm\frac{a}{b}\right).$$

The sign of μ_1 and μ_2 depends on the sign of the scale factor of the transformation Φ.

Problem 142. Show that' ${\Phi_{n2}}^{-1}\Phi_{n1}$ is an enlargement with centre M', and deduce the method shown in Figure 98 for constructing points on an ellipse from points of the circles on its axes.

Draw in the tangents to the curves at the three related points P_1, P_2 and P'.

We now wish to show that every ellipse Γ′ can be obtained as a plane section of a circular cylinder. According to Problem 141 there exists a normal affinity Φ_{n2} which maps the circle Γ_2 on the minor axis onto Γ′; the scale factor of the affinity being

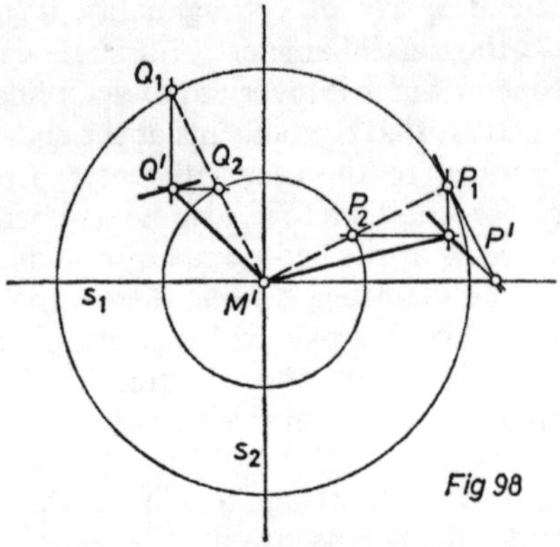

Fig 98

a/b. We now imagine the ellipse Γ' turned out of its plane. We choose s_2, the axis of Φ_{n2}, as the axis of rotation and make the angle of rotation $\phi = \cos^{-1} b/a$. The points P_2 and P', which were corresponding points under Φ_{n2}, will, after this rotation, lie on a line orthogonal to the plane of the circle Γ_2. Hence, the ellipse now lies on the cylinder over the circle Γ_2 (see Figure 99).

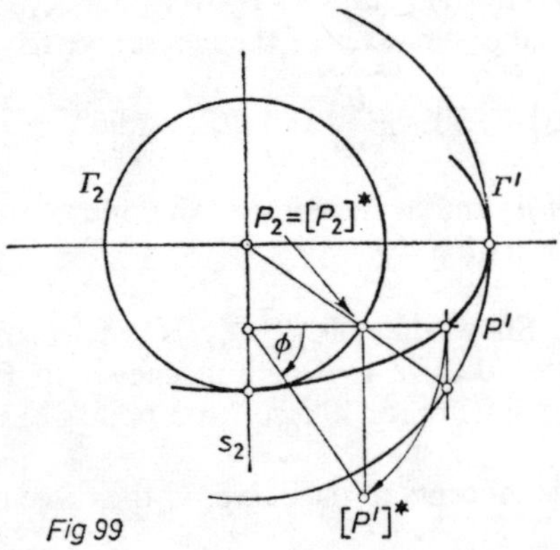

Fig 99

Problem 143. Show that the ellipse is the locus of all points whose distances from two fixed points F_1 and F_2 have a constant sum.

We use the fact that every ellipse can be obtained as the intersection of a plane ε with a circular cylinder.

Imagine that we take two spheres of radius b and push them into the cylinder from opposite ends until they touch the plane ε. Let the two points of contact be F_1 and F_2. It is then easy to show that for all points P' on the ellipse the sum $P'F_1+P'F_2$ has a constant value. The generating line of the cylinder through P' touches the two spheres in points A and B. We now use the fact that all tangents from a point P' to a sphere have the same length. Hence, we obtain

$$P'F_1+P'F_2 = P'A+P'B = AB.$$

AB is the segment of the generating line through P' which is bounded by the two circles of contact between the spheres and the cylinder. It can be seen immediately that AB does not depend upon the position of the point P' on the ellipse.*

The two points F_1 and F_2 are known as the *foci of the ellipse.*

Problem 143 introduced an important metric property of the ellipse. Here, however, we are mainly interested in the affine properties of ellipses and the following theorem takes us back once more to affine geometry.

Theorem 19. A pair of conjugate diameters determines exactly one ellipse.

The content of this theorem is not trivial since a pair of conjugate diameters can be mapped onto orthogonal line segments having equal length, by infinitely many affinities. It is not immediately obvious that the inverse transformations will always map the circle onto the same ellipse.

We prove this by giving a construction for an ellipse starting with a pair of conjugate diameters. It is necessary that this construction is an affine invariant, that is, is built up from affine invariant operations such as drawing parallels, or dividing line segments in given ratios. We do not allow such operations as drawing right-angles.

Let AB be a diameter of the circle Γ (see Figure 100), C a

* This method of proof is due to G. P. Dandelin (1794-1847). The two spheres appearing in the proof are sometimes called Dandelin's spheres.

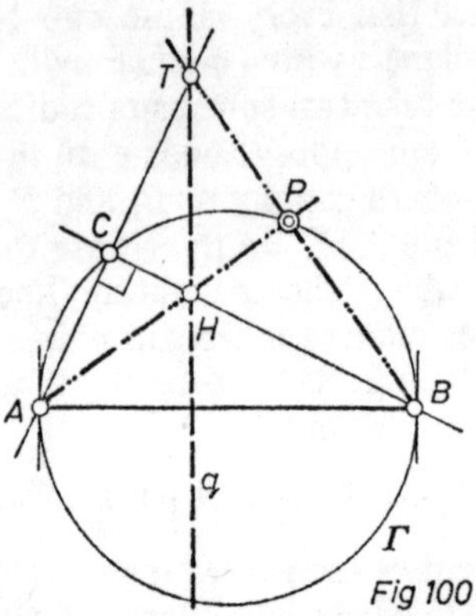

Fig 100

point on Γ, and q an arbitrary perpendicular to AB. Since C lies on the circle, $\angle ACB = 90°$. We now extend AC until it meets q and we letter this point T. H is the orthocentre of the triangle ABT. The line AP is the third altitude and is, therefore, perpendicular to BT. We conclude that P, the point of intersection of the lines BT and AH, lies on Γ. If we let q move (still, however, remaining perpendicular to AB), then P will describe the whole circle. Hence, Figure 100 shows a construction which allows us to find any number of points on a circle without using compasses, provided a diameter and one other point of the circle are given. Consequently we can solve the following problem without using compasses:

Problem 144. Given two mutually orthogonal diameters AB and CD of a circle Γ, construct the point of intersection of Γ with a line g through B.

The solution is given in Figure 101(a).

Apart from drawing the right-angle between q and AB all the steps in the construction are affine. We can, however, interpret the construction completely in affine invariant terms, if we interpret q not as the perpendicular to AB, but as a parallel to the tangents to the circle at A and B (that is, q is the conjugate direction to AB). It should be mentioned that P can be obtained directly by drawing the perpendicular to g through A.

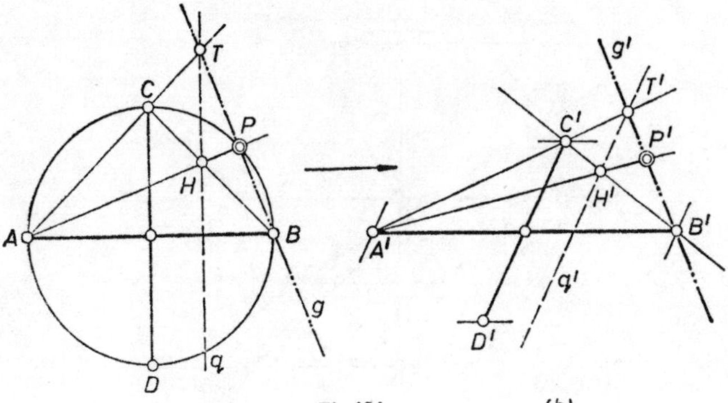

Fig 101

However, the affine nature of the construction is lost by this short cut.

An affine translation changes Figure 101(a) into Figure 101(b).

We can now base the proof of our uniqueness theorem on Figure 101. If a given pair of conjugate diameters $A'B'$ and $C'D'$ is mapped by a perspective affinity onto an orthogonal pair AB, CD which have the same length (the position of the axis of affinity is irrelevant), then the inverse mapping applied to the circle construction shown in Figure 101(a) always produces the same image. The reason for this is that all the points and lines constructed in Figure 101(b) depend only on the given pair of conjugate diameters. The position of P' on g' is, therefore, uniquely determined. If we now rotate g' round the point B', then P' describes a well-defined curve—the ellipse with the given conjugate diameters.*

Problem 145. The mid-point of the line segment HT in Figure 101(a) lies on the tangents to the circle Γ through C and P. Use this property to obtain a construction for drawing tangents to an ellipse.

* The remarkable configuration of Figure 100, on which this proof is based, is given in Volume 3 of *Enzyklopädie der Elementarmathematik* by Weber-Wellstein. It is a special case of Pascal's Theorem.

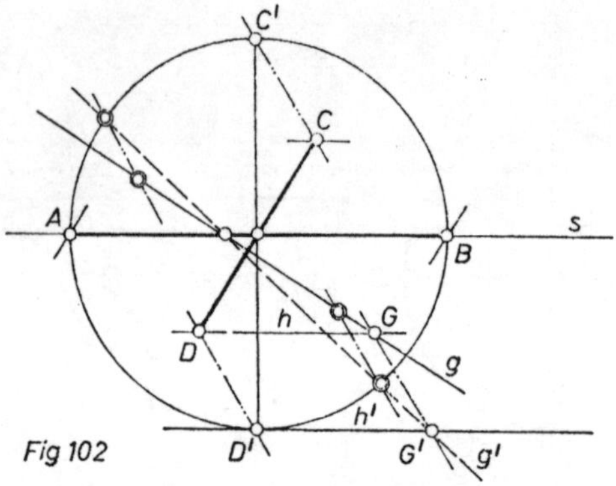

Fig 102

Problem 146. An ellipse is given by means of a pair of conjugate diameters. Determine the points of intersection of the ellipse with an arbitrary line g.

We mention this simple problem on ellipses because its solution introduces a new means of using transformation geometry.

The given ellipse can be mapped onto a circle by an affinity. The simplest mapping to use is one which leaves one of the conjugate diameters invariant. That is, we consider a perspective affinity Φ which has one of the two diameters as its axis of affinity. The line g is mapped onto g' by Φ. Now the problem has been transformed into one concerning a circle. We have to find the points of intersection of g' with the image circle and then construct the images of these two points under the mapping Φ^{-1} (see Figure 102).

In this problem we meet an idea which is frequently used in higher mathematics. A given problem is reduced by means of a suitable transformation to a simpler case for which the solution is already known or at least obtainable more easily. The solution of the general case is then obtained by considering the image of the simpler solution under the inverse transformation. This is an extremely useful method of solution.

The following problem can be solved in the same way.

Problem 147. Two ellipses are given whose major and minor axes are parallel and in the same ratio. Find their points of intersection.

An affinity which transforms one ellipse into a circle will also map the second ellipse onto a circle. Hence, a suitable affinity reduces the problem to that of finding the points of intersection of two circles.

Problem 148. Construct an ellipse which has the given diameter AB and passes through two given points P and Q.

An ellipse can be constructed if it can be represented as the affine image of a circle. Hence, we have to find a perspective affinity which maps the required ellipse onto a suitable circle.

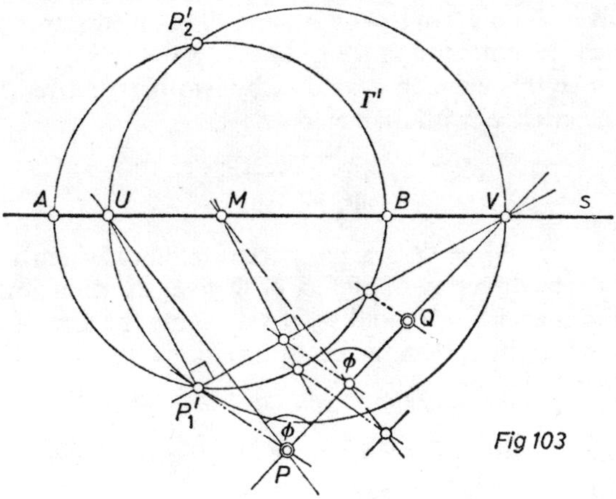

Fig 103

We take the line AB to be the axis of affinity of our mapping. In a circle every chord is orthogonal to the line joining its mid-point to the centre of the circle. The equivalent property for an ellipse is that a chord and the line joining its mid-point to the centre of the ellipse define conjugate directions. Therefore we have to choose the affinity in such a way that the angle ϕ (see Figure 103) is transformed into a right-angle. If we translate the angle ϕ to P we have, together with the circle with diameter AB, two geometric loci for P' (since P' lies on the circle with UV as diameter). Hence, we obtain two solutions for P'—the points P_1' and P_2'. Correspondingly there are two affinities

Φ_1 and Φ_2 to be considered. We now want to show that both affinities map Γ' onto the same ellipse, that is, there is only one ellipse with the required properties.

We note that P_2' is obtained from P_1' by the reflection M_s. For the inverse transformations we therefore have

$$\Phi_2^{-1} = \Phi_1^{-1}M_s.$$

However, the reflection M_s leaves Γ' invariant, hence, the image of Γ' is the same for Φ_1^{-1} and Φ_2^{-1}. Thus the problem has a unique solution.

Problem 149. Two ellipses e_1 and e_2 have a common diameter AB. Given P on e_1 and Q on e_2, and the tangents at P and Q, construct the common tangents to the two curves.

To solve this we map e_1 and e_2 by two perspective affinities onto the circle e' with diameter AB:

$$e_1 \xrightarrow[\Phi_1]{} e' \xleftarrow[\Phi_2]{} e_2.$$

Then $\Phi_2^{-1}\Phi_1 = \Phi$ is a perspective affinity which maps e_1 onto e_2. The direction of affinity of Φ gives the direction of the common tangents of e_1 and e_2. If we denote the axis of affinity of Φ_1 and Φ_2 by s, then the transformations

$$\Phi_1' = M_s\Phi_1 \quad \text{and} \quad \Phi_2' = M_s\Phi_2$$

also map e_1 and e_2 onto the circle e'. Since we have

$$\Phi_2'^{-1}\Phi_1' = (M_s\Phi_2)^{-1}M_s\Phi_1 = \Phi_2^{-1}M_sM_s\Phi_1 = \Phi_2^{-1}\Phi_1,$$

this combination produces the same affine relation between e_1 and e_2. The four possible combinations of Φ_1, Φ_1' and Φ_2, Φ_2' produce only two different transformations; to each of these corresponds two common tangents of e_1 and e_2.

Problem 150. Show that all ellipses belong to the same equivalence class with respect to $\mathfrak{Q}$.

BIBLIOGRAPHY

The bibliography of the German edition listed 16 books of which the following are published in English.

KLEIN, F., *Elementary Mathematics from an Advanced Standpoint* (Vol. 2, Geometry), Macmillan, New York, 1939.

WEYL, H., *Symmetry*, Princeton University Press, Princeton, 1952.

An O-level course based on transformation geometry can be found in the textbooks of the S.M.P. In Book T the emphasis is on construction problems involving a single transformation—the transformations considered are the isometries (excluding glide-reflection), enlargements and shears. Book T4 introduces products of transformations and the glide-reflection. The group properties of transformations are not developed but an account is given of the description in matrix terms of transformations having a fixed point. Similar work on transformation matrices is contained in Matthews. The Teacher's Guide to Book T has a valuable section on motion geometry which will certainly be of great assistance to any teacher who wishes to try out this approach to geometry. Further guidance on class-room presentation is contained in Chapter 10 of the A.T.M. handbook (this also mentions some of the group applications).

Rather more advanced accounts of the subject can be found in two Russian translations: Yaglom, in which only isometries are considered, and Kutuzov. Coxeter in his excellent, comprehensive book gives a short but readable account of the various groups of transformations.

A footnote on p. 43 tells the reader where information on the description of patterns and figures in group theoretical terms can be found. Terpstra's pamphlet is intended to supplement Escher's collection of designs and these, together with the books by Weyl and Wells, make fascinating reading. A readable and inexpensive approach to symmetry and plane patterns is given by Bell and Fletcher. The work on cycles of half-turns and reflections on p. 72 is also done by Thomsen (but this article is now of interest mainly from a historical point of view) and a full scale axiomatic treatment of this group theoretic approach to geometry can be found in Bachmann (German).

Readers to whom group theory is new should follow up one or two of the ideas hinted at in this book. A more detailed account of cosets (the name given to the sets appearing in the decomposition of $\mathfrak{G}_8$ on p. 78) and a proof of Lagrange's Theorem (here stated without proof) can be found in any book on groups. One of the cheapest and most readable is Ledermann. Problem 109 has deep implications in group theory as the reader will discover if he investigates normal and conjugate subgroups. An exciting, but expensive, treatment of groups is given by Papy.

A.T.M. HANDBOOK, *Some Lessons in Mathematics*, Cambridge University Press, London, 1964.

BACHMANN, F., *Aufbau der Geometrie aus dem Spiegelungsbegriff*, (Grundlehren der mathematischen Wissenschaften, 96), Springer, Berlin, 1959.

BELL A. and FLETCHER T. J., *Symmetry Groups*, A.T.M. Mathematics Teaching Pamphlet No. 12, 1964.

COXETER, H. S. M., *Introduction to Geometry*, New York, London, Wiley, 1961.

ESCHER, M. C, *The Graphic work of M. C. Escher*, Oldbourne Press, London, 1961.

KUTUZOV, B. B., *Geometry*, (Studies in Mathematics, 4), School Mathematics Study Group, New Haven (Conn.) 1960.

LEDERMANN, W., *Introduction to the Theory of Finite Groups*, Oliver and Boyd, Edinburgh, 1949.

MATTHEWS, G., *Matrices* (2 vols.), Arnold, London, 1964.

PAPY, G., *Groups*, Macmillan, London, 1964.

SCHOOL MATHEMATICS PROJECT, *Book T*, Cambridge University Press, London, 1964.

SCHOOL MATHEMATICS PROJECT, *Teacher's Guide for Book T*, Cambridge University Press, London, 1965.

SCHOOL MATHEMATICS PROJECT, *Book T4*, Cambridge University Press, London, 1965.

SCHOOL MATHEMATICS PROJECT, *Teacher's Guide for Book T4*, Cambridge University Press, London, 1966.

TERPSTRA, P., *Some notes on the Mathematical Background of Repetitive Patterns*, Oldbourne Press, London, 1961.

THOMSEN, G., "The Treatment of Elementary Geometry by a Group-calculus", *Mathematical Gazette*, 17, No. 224 (October 1933), pp. 230-42.

WELLS, A. F., *The Third Dimension in Chemistry*, Clarendon Press, Oxford, 1956.

YAGLOM, I. M., *Geometric Transformations*, Random House, New York, 1962.